NEW TESTAMENT MESSAGE

A Biblical-Theological Commentary

Wilfrid Harrington, O.P. and Donald Senior, C.P.
EDITORS

New Testament Message, Volume 22

THE APOCALYPSE

Adela Yarbro Collins

A Michael Glazier Book
THE LITURGICAL PRESS
Collegeville, Minnesota

About the Author

Adela Yarbro Collins is an Associate Professor of New Testament at McCormick Theological Seminary in Chicago. She studied New Testament and Theology at the University of Tuebingen in West Germany and received a Ph.D. from Harvard University. She is an Associate Editor of the Catholic Biblical Quarterly. Her published works include her dissertation, *The Combat Myth in the Book of Revelation*, and articles in the *Catholic Biblical Quarterly*, the *Journal of Biblical Literature*, the *Harvard Theological Review*, the *Catholic Charismatic, Chicago Studies*, and *Theology Digest*.

A Michael Glazier Book published by The Liturgical Press

Library of Congress Catalog Card Number: 79-52926
ISBN 0-8146-5145-3

6   7   8   9   10

CONTENTS

To my parents,
Dr. and Mrs. Jesse L. Yarbro,
with
love and gratitude.

EDITORS' PREFACE

New Testament Message is a commentary series designed to bring the best of biblical scholarship to a wide audience. Anyone who is sensitive to the mood of the church today is aware of a deep craving for the Word of God. This interest in reading and praying the scriptures is not confined to a religious elite. The desire to strengthen one's faith and to mature in prayer has brought Christians of all types and all ages to discover the beauty of the biblical message. Our age has also been heir to an avalanche of biblical scholarship. Recent archaeological finds, new manuscript evidence, and the increasing volume of specialized studies on the Bible have made possible a much more profound penetration of the biblical message. But the flood of information and its technical nature keeps much of this scholarship out of the hands of the Christian who is eager to learn but is not a specialist. *New Testament Message* is a response to this need.

The subtitle of the series is significant: "A Biblical-Theological Commentary." Each volume in the series, while drawing on up-to-date scholarship, concentrates on bringing to the fore in understandable terms the specific message of each biblical author. The essay-format (rather than a word-by-word commentary) helps the reader savor the beauty and power of the biblical message and, at the same time, understand the sensitive task of responsible biblical interpretation.

A distinctive feature of the series is the amount of space given to the "neglected" New Testament writings, such as Colossians, James, Jude, the Pastoral Letters, the Letters of Peter and John. These briefer biblical books make a significant but often overlooked contribution to the richness of the New Testament. By assigning larger than normal coverage to these books, the series hopes to give these parts of Scripture the attention they deserve.

Because *New Testament Message* is aimed at the entire English speaking world, it is a collaborative effort of international proportions. The twenty-two contributors represent biblical scholarship in North America, Britain, Ireland and Australia. Each of the contributors is a recognized expert in his or her field, has published widely, and has been chosen because of a proven ability to communicate at a popular level. And, while all of the contributors are Roman Catholic, their work is addressed to the Christian community as a whole. The New Testament is the patrimony of all Christians.It is the hope of all concerned with this series that it will bring a fuller appreciation of God's saving Word to his people.

Wilfrid Harrington, O.P.
Donald Senior, C.P.

INTRODUCTION

LIKE THE SCROLL which the Lamb takes from the enthroned one in chapter five, the Apocalypse itself might as well be sealed with seven seals for many in the church today. There is a variety of reasons for this situation. For some the book simply does not make sense. It has no plot and there is no apparent logic in the order of the episodes. While some of the images are vaguely familiar from the Old Testament, most are opaque and originate in a strange, foreign world. Other people think of the Apocalypse seldom and with distaste because they associate it with the literal expectation of a speedy end to the world held by various millennarian sects. Commercially successful and sensational books seem to play upon this expectation and rather implausibly identify characters in the Apocalypse with current people and nations. Still others hold the Apocalypse in low esteem because of its fervent hope that the blood of the martyrs will be avenged by the bloody destruction of their enemies. They feel that this "blood for blood" attitude is a step backward from Jesus' teaching that one should love one's enemies. For example, Alfred North Whitehead expressed regret that this book has influence on the formation of religious sentiment because of its "barbaric elements." D. H. Lawrence attacked the Apocalypse as an outgrowth and reinforcement of envy on the part of the "have-nots," as their spiteful attack on all the pleasures and achievements of human civilization.

The interpretation of the Apocalypse offered in this volume is intended to respond to these problems and criticisms. It hopes to show that there is a distinctive and powerful logic which relates the various parts of the Apocalypse to each other. Its images also can be made more translucent. Further, the writer hopes to show people attracted or repelled by the millennarian interpretation that the Apocalypse does not provide a timetable of the end of the world; its purpose is quite different. On the other hand, it must be admitted that the book does not evoke a religious sentiment as deeply challenging as Jesus' command to love your enemies and pray for those who persecute you. That command and others like it, however, have proved notoriously difficult to implement as a blueprint for christian life. There is the further problem of the selective application of such sayings in society and even in the church. Only certain people are really expected to "turn the other cheek." Given these problems, one might say that the love command of Jesus, embodied in the gospels, was providentially complemented in the formation of the New Testament canon by the call for justice contained in the Apocalypse.

This interpretation is written in the conviction that the key to understanding a work is its literary form. The goals and methods of an editorial are very different from those of a news story. Misunderstanding will result if a reader brings inappropriate expectations to a work. Apoc 1:4-5 and 22:21 seem to mark the Apocalypse as a letter. But the preface (1:1-3) and the rest of the book show that whoever tries to read it as a letter will be severely frustrated. Actually, the work is an "apocalypse," a revelatory narrative. It tells how the prophet John received revelatory visions from Christ and it describes the visions themselves. To a large extent, the visions concern the future, but they were written down in order to illuminate the present experience of the author and the first readers and to evoke a particular response to that experience. The author, probably the prophet himself, made use of traditional images in describing his visions. He did so in such a way that they express a view of reality which is still powerful today. The presence of traditional images in this case is a sign that the Apocalypse is a kind of allegorical narrative. As is usual in such narrative, there are two levels of meaning. One level is the "old story" evoked by the traditional images. The other level is the "new story" which is the substance of the narrative itself.

The "old story" evoked by the traditional images in the Apocalypse is the ancient story of cosmic combat. Actually there were many stories of combat in the ancient Mediterranean world, but they shared certain basic features. The story usually begins with the rebellion of a divine or cosmic beast against the young creator god who maintains order in nature and among people. Sometimes the beast, often a dragon, wins at first, but ultimately the hero-god is victorious and re-establishes order in the world. The power and meaning of these stories cannot be reduced to a single interpretation or even expressed very well in abstract concepts. They grasp the imagination, evoke a response and have many connotations. St. George battling the dragon is a story of this type which has remained in living memory up to the present. One important function of these stories is to express in a vivid and concrete way the perennial struggle between life and death, fertility and sterility, order and chaos. The dragon, for example, is a powerful symbol of the chaotic force which threatens to disrupt nature and destroy humanity.

The "new story" of the Apocalypse is concerned with the confrontation between the followers of Jesus and the Roman empire. The expected hostility on the part of Rome is interpreted as the rebellion of chaos against divine order. The polarity in the natural world expressed by the combat story is associated in the "new story" of the Apocalypse primarily with human society and the supernatural realm. The new polarity borders on dualism. All humanity is divided into followers of Christ and worshipers of the Roman empire (13:8). The Roman emperor is described as an Antichrist (compare 13:1-3 with 5:6 and 19:12-13). It is implied that Satan rebels against God (13:6, 20:7-10). This polarity expressed and reinforced the fundamental alienation of the prophet John and probably his first readers from the political order determined by Rome and even from the world as they experienced it. The worshipers of Rome are equated with the dwellers on earth (13:8). A basic solidarity of the earth with the social realm is presumed. Thus the earth must be destroyed before the new age can dawn (21:1).

The Apocalypse, however, does not reflect a total alienation from the created world. Strange as it sounds, one who is totally alienated from the world would not be so concerned about its destruction. A more thorough-going disenchantment with the world is expressed in certain gnostic writings, where the main concern is how the individual can escape from the world and enjoy a purely spiritual or heavenly existence. The Apocalypse is interested in overcoming alienation from the world. This alienation cannot be overcome fully in the present, but there are indications that the Apocalypse expects it to be overcome partially in this age.

These indications can be found in the way the book is composed. One of the major problems for the interpretation of the Apocalypse has long been how to understand the apparent repetitions. For example, the end is described at least twice (11:15-19 and 19:11-22:5); the salvation of the just is likewise repeated (7:9-17 and 21:3-8). One point of view is that the doublets result from the combining of various written sources. This point of view was very popular around the turn of the century. It has been largely discredited because of the overall unity of language and style in the Apocalypse. The other point of view is that the repetitions are part of the design of the author. Those who hold this point of view differ on whether events are described in linear progression or in a purposely repetitive way. The linear theory works only if one concedes that certain visions provide a preview of the end (like 7:9-17 and 11:15-19). But this concession already gives up to a large extent the idea of a linear development. The theory of purposeful repetition is the most illuminating. This theory is often called the "recapitulation theory," and it was first proposed in the patristic period.

The revelation of the future begins in 6:1. The visions which follow are organized into five series as the following table shows:

1. The seven seals	6:1 - 8:5
2. The seven trumpets	8:2 -11:19

3. Seven unnumbered visions   12:1 -15:4
4. The seven bowls   15:1 -16:20
    Babylon appendix   17:1-19:10
5. Seven unnumbered visions   19:11-21:8
    Jerusalem appendix   21:9-22:5

Each of these series describes events which have the same basic pattern. That common pattern has three elements: (1) persecution, (2) punishment of the nations or judgment, and (3) triumph of God, the Lamb and his followers or salvation. The following chart shows where these elements appear in each of the five series of visions:

1. The seven seals
    persecution   6:9-11
    judgment   6:12-17
    triumph   7:9-17
2. The seven trumpets
    allusion to persecution   8:3-5
    allusion to judgment   9:15
    triumph   11:15-19
3. Seven unnumbered visions
    persecution   12-13
                 (especially 13:7-10)
    judgment   14:14-20
    triumph   15:2-4
4. The seven bowls
    persecution   16:4-7
    judgment   16:17-20
    triumph   19:1-10
5. Seven unnumbered visions
    persecution   20:9
    judgment   20:9-15
    triumph   21:1-22:5

To the modern reader, who expects a clear, orderly progression in narrative accounts, this recapitulation is confusing. But it does seem to have a specific purpose and to fulfill that purpose remarkably well. The Apocalypse is attempting to express something inexpressible. No single attempt is adequate. Each formulation points beyond itself to a mysterious quality of reality. The several formulations (the five series of visions) taken together are a more adequate expression of the mystery than any one of them alone. It would seem then that the specific details of the visions are of secondary importance. It is the basic, underlying pattern of persecution, judgment and salvation that is the real message of the Apocalypse.

What is that message? The traditional images of combat reveal that reality is deeply characterized by conflict and struggle. They also show death as a phase in the cosmic struggle, not the end. This claim is reinforced by the example of Jesus. The story of combat and the story about Jesus function as models for understanding and coming to terms with powerlessness, suffering and death. Such experiences are an inevitable part of reality for reasons which cannot be expressed directly and abstractly. But the Apocalypse does not advocate a passive and fatalistic acceptance of these misfortunes. It tried to illuminate the situation in which it was written, to distinguish between the affairs of God and those of Satan. The reader is challenged to make an analogous judgment on one's own world and to live one's life deeply committed to the current expressions of God's cause. The message of the Apocalypse is that misfortunes endured in a life so committed are not in vain. The powers of creation and destruction are very nearly matched. Nevertheless, the forces of creation do have the edge. Reality is conditioned by them more deeply and more truly.

The Apocalypse thus makes a claim on its readers. It calls them to view the world in a certain way and to allow their lives to be shaped by that outlook. The book wants to shape not only individuals but communities and the world as well. We will examine the particularities of the Apocalypse's claim on its readers as we look more closely at the book itself.

Part I
THE SEALED SCROLL.
1-11.

MANY COMMENTATORS have noted that the Apocalypse seems to be divided into two parts, chapters 1-11 and 12-22. The seven trumpets are closely linked with the seven seals, because the appearance of the angels who will blow the trumpets is the result of the opening of the seventh seal (8:1-2). When the seventh trumpet is blown, however, there is a natural break (11:15-19). Near the beginning of the first half of the book, John has a vision of Christ who gives him revelation and commissions him to deliver it to others (1:9-3:22). The revelation is continued in the following portion with the opening of the scroll with seven seals. Near the end of the first half, John has a vision of an angel who gives him further revelation and commissions him once more to deliver it to others (chapter 10). The commission (10:11) makes clear that the content of the revelation is revealed in chapters 12-22. Thus each half of the book is related to a commissioning vision and to a scroll. The first half is characterized by the scroll with seven seals introduced in chapter 5. The second half is associated with the little scroll which was lying open in the hand of the angel (10:2) and which he gave John to eat (10:8-10). The description of the first scroll as sealed reflects the fragmentary and heavily veiled character of chapters 1-11 with regard to the situation being addressed and the expected outcome. In the second half of the book the situation and its outcome are clarified. The increased clarity is reflected in the description of the second scroll as open in the angel's hand.

A. PROLOGUE.
1:1-8.

THE BODY of the Apocalypse consists of a narrative account in the first person in which John describes his revelatory experiences (1:9-22:5). This central narrative is framed by miscellaneous introductory (1:1-8) and concluding material (22:6-21).

THE TITLE.
1:1-2.

> 1 The revelation of Jesus Christ, which God gave him to show to his servants what must soon take place; and he made it known by sending his angel to his servant John, ²who bore witness to the word of God and to the testimony of Jesus Christ, even to all that he saw.

These words seem to serve as a descriptive title of the work as a whole. It is *revelation;* the same Greek word is sometimes translated "revelation" and sometimes "apocalypse." It means literally an unveiling of a previously hidden truth or reality. This revelation is of heavenly origin. It is not something human beings can arrive at through observation or reflection. The Apocalypse is not based on a point of view compatible with a natural theology. Rather, it presupposes that human beings are incapable of arriving at true understanding by their own efforts and that creation is alienated from the creator. So a person must be receptive to divine revelatory activity which grasps one from outside oneself. The mysteriousness of that divine revelatory activity is shown by its indirect character. It originates in a distant and hidden *God* who communicates with *his servants* through *Jesus Christ.* Even Jesus does not communicate directly with each of his followers, but he sends *his angel* to *John,* who finally bears *witness* to the other believers concerning what he has seen and heard.

PRELIMINARY BLESSING.
1:3.

> ³Blessed is he who reads aloud the words of the prophecy, and blessed are those who hear, and who keep what is written therein; for the time is near.

This is the first of seven beatitudes in the Apocalypse (1:3, 14:13, 16:15, 19:9, 20:6, 22:7 and 14). This one proclaims fortunate the one who *reads* the book *aloud,* those who *hear* it read, and those who *keep* what is written, that is, who live in accordance with the book. This preliminary blessing is balanced by a shorter one in the epilogue, which praises those who *keep* what is written in the book (22:7). The blessedness or happiness is the result of the gift of divine revelation and its acceptance.

Apparently the Apocalypse was read aloud to the whole congregation. The reading may have taken place at the regular worship service or people may have gathered especially to hear it. Here the book is referred to as a *prophecy.* The author does not seem to have distinguished between an apocalyptic and a prophetic book. Most modern commentators do, however. One difference has to do with how God is perceived. In the prophetic oracles, God is very near and speaks directly to his servants the prophets. In apocalyptic works, as here, God is not so accessible, but is a more hidden and mysterious being.

JOHN ADDRESSES HIS READERS.
1:4-8.

> 4John to the seven churches that are in Asia:
> Grace to you and peace from him who is and who
> was and who is to come, and from the seven spirits who
> are before his throne, 5and from Jesus Christ the faith-
> ful witness, the first-born of the dead, and the ruler of
> kings on earth.
>
> To him who loves us and has freed us from our sins
> by his blood 6and made us a kingdom, priests to his
> God and Father, to him be glory and dominion for-
> ever and ever. Amen. 7Behold, he is coming with the
> clouds, and every eye will see him, every one who pierced
> him; and all tribes of the earth will wail on account
> of him. Even so. Amen.
>
> 8"I am the Alpha and the Omega," says the Lord
> God, who is and who was and who is to come, the
> Almighty.

The first part of verse 4 is an example of the salutation
of a typical ancient letter. The sender is mentioned first
and then the intended receiver of the letter. As noted in
the introduction, the body of the Apocalypse is better
understood as an apocalyptic narrative than as a letter.
Even though the letter form is used only superficially,
its use is important. It shows that the book was written
with a specific audience in mind. Only when they received
it would the process of revelation be complete (see 1:2
and 11).

Since the book was to be sent to more than one church,
it seems to have been a circular letter. There has been much
speculation about why exactly *seven* churches were
addressed and why the particular ones mentioned in 1:11.
There are many logical possibilities. The most probable
reason for the number *seven* is its symbolic character.
Since it is a prime number, both Greeks and Jews considered it a symbol of perfection and plenitude. Thus
seven particular churches could represent the whole

Church. The selection of these particular churches was most probably due to their positions on a major road. Each of them could serve as a central point for further circulation of the book.

In the second part of verse 4 and the first part of verse 5, we find a greeting, which is another typical element in an ancient letter. The wish for *grace* is a particularly christian element, but the prayer for *peace* is also found in Jewish letters of the time. It is striking that John dares to give this greeting in the names of God and *Jesus Christ.* This indirect claim to be a mediator is also found in the greetings of Paul's letters (see, for example, Romans 1:7). In referring to *the seven spirits,* John is probably taking over the Jewish tradition of the seven archangels. Such an idea is part of the increasing sense of the hiddenness of God; God is not directly involved in the affairs of the world, but has created intermediary beings who are active in the world.

Near the end of the greeting, Jesus is given several titles. One of these is *the faithful witness.* The Greek word for "witness" is the same one which later on has the technical sense of "martyr." The word has its roots in the courtroom —a witness is one who gives evidence before a judge. It is easy to see how the word came to mean someone who dies for the faith. In the Roman persecutions, a Christian would usually be given a trial before being executed. Here "witness" is not yet a technical term. It still has its primary sense of giving verbal testimony. Its use here probably refers to the message of Jesus given in his whole ministry. But it also evokes the courtroom setting and makes the reader think of the arrest, trial and death of Jesus. This allusion to a legal trial is significant given the situation of the first readers, as we shall see.

The other two titles make outrageous claims about Jesus from the point of view of the disinterested observer. While many Jews hoped for a future resurrection of the righteous as a group, the claim that a single individual had already been raised from the dead seemed far-fetched to most. The idea that an obscure teacher and wonder-worker from Galilee, who had been executed as a criminal in the most degrading way known to Roman law, is actually *the ruler of kings on earth* must have seemed preposterous to the average citizen of the Roman empire.

In the second part of verse 5 and in verse 6 we find a doxology directed toward Jesus. The theme of Jesus' *love* of the believers appears only here and in 3:9. This theme is one of several shared by the Apocalypse and the gospel of John. The *freeing from sins by his blood* is probably a traditional element which interprets Jesus' death in terms of the theology of sacrifice. Jesus is said to have made the believers a *kingdom* and *priests to God* in verse 6. Here the work of Jesus is seen as a fulfillment of an old promise (see Ex 19:6). That the believers are a *kingdom* means that they have recognized God's rule over them, not that they themselves are rulers already. That they are *priests* means that they are now the legitimate mediators between the creator and the creation.

In verses 7 and 8 we find two prophetic sayings. The first is a combination of Dan 7:13 and Zech 12:10. The same combination is found in Mt 24:30. In the context of the Apocalypse, the saying expresses John's conviction that the whole world will one day be forced to recognize the truth of the outrageous claims made about Jesus in the greeting. The second saying (verse 8) concludes the prologue. It has the traditional prophetic form-[thus] *says the Lord God . . . .* This is the first of only two occasions in the whole Apocalypse when it is clear that a saying is presented as God's own words. The other is 21:5-8. Here God is presented as saying, "*I am the Alpha and the Omega.*" *Alpha* and *Omega* are the first and last letters of the Greek alphabet. They are used here symbolically to mean "first" and "last," or "beginning" and "end" (see 21:6 and 22:13). In the context of 1:8, the saying points to God as the source and the fulfillment of all things. This aspect of the symbols is highlighted by the title *who is and who was and who is to come.* A reader with a mystical or somewhat static understanding of reality expects the third element of the title to be *and who will be*. But the Apocalypse does not present a static view of God or of reality. God is not simply One who is, but One who comes; God, however distant and hidden, is still one who breaks into human experience in unexpected and surprising ways.

John's address to his readers (1:4-8) is similar to the openings of Paul's letters. Paul usually began with a salutation, greeting and a doxology or thanksgiving which ended with an expression of hope (see, for example, 1 Cor 1:1-9). Like Paul in 1 Cor 1:9, John ends his introductory remarks with a saying which refers to the source of all being and, specifically, the source of christian faith and hope.

B. JOHN GIVES AN ACCOUNT OF HIS INAUGURAL VISION AND COMMISSION TO WRITE.
1:9 - 3:22.

THIS WHOLE SECTION is, in terms of form, a vision account. With it the body of the Apocalypse begins, an apocalyptic narrative. The inaugural vision, 1:9 - 3:22, might more accurately be called an epiphany, because it is primarily an appearance or manifestation of the risen Christ. The content of the revelation is not so much what is *seen* as what is *said* by the revealing figure, Christ. This verbal revelation is contained in the seven messages of chapters 2 and 3.

AN EPIPHANY OF THE SON OF MAN.
1:9-20.

⁹I John, your brother, who share with you in Jesus the tribulation and the kingdom and the patient endurance, was on the island called Patmos on account of the word of God and the testimony of Jesus. ¹⁰I was in the Spirit on the Lord's day, and I heard behind me a loud voice like a trumpet ¹¹saying, "Write what you see in a book and send it to the seven churches, to Ephesus and to Smyrna and to Pergamum and to Thyatira and to Sardis and to Philadelphia and to Laodicea."

¹²Then I turned to see the voice that was speaking to me, and on turning I saw seven golden lampstands, ¹³and

in the midst of the lampstands one like a son of man,
clothed with a long robe and with a golden girdle round
his breast; [14]his head and his hair were white as wool,
white as snow; his eyes were like a flame of fire, [15]his feet
were like burnished bronze, refined as in a furnace, and
his voice was like the sound of many waters; [16]in his right
hand he held seven stars, from his mouth issued a sharp
two-edged sword, and his face was like the sun shining in
full strength.

[17]When I saw him, I fell at his feet as though dead.
But he laid his right hand upon me, saying, "Fear not, I
am the first and the last, [18]and the living one, I died, and
behold I am alive for evermore, and I have the keys of
Death and Hades. [19]Now write what you see, what is and
what is to take place hereafter. [20]As for the mystery of the
seven stars which you saw in my right hand, and the seven
golden lampstands, the seven stars are the angels of the
seven churches and the seven lampstands are the seven
churches.

The linking of *the tribulation and the kingdom and the
patient endurance* is striking. The idea expressed here is
similar to the point of view of one of the sayings of Jesus
(Mt 11:12), "From the days of John the Baptist until now
the kingdom of heaven has suffered violence, and men of
violence take it by force." Both passages presuppose the
apocalyptic idea that, in the present, there is a struggle going
on between the kingdom of God and the kingdom of Satan.
Ultimately the victory belongs to God, but in the present
Satan is in control. This point of view reflects the old story
of combat discussed in the introduction. For a time, the
dragon wins. For John, membership in the kingdom of God
had meant banishment for a time to Patmos, a tiny island
off the coast of Asia Minor, modern Turkey. A few decades
later, execution of any confessing Christian was the rule
in that region. The fate of Antipas (2:13) shows that such
executions were already carried out in John's time. That
John was banished rather than executed may be a sign of
his social status, perhaps Roman citizenship.

John describes his visionary experience with language and imagery typical of vision accounts in apocalyptic literature. His *falling as though dead* and needing to be revived are typical features which emphasize the overwhelming and otherworldly character of the revelatory experience. The interpretation by the revealer of the *seven stars* and *the seven golden lampstands*, mysterious elements in the vision itself, is another typical feature. These literary conventions do not exclude the possibility that the account reflects an actual ecstatic experience. They may, on the contrary, result from the regular features of such experiences. It is clear, however, that whatever actually happened to John, he expressed and interpreted his experience in terms of the tradition with which he was familiar and of the world in which he lived.

The *seven golden lampstands* are interpreted in 1:20 as the *seven churches*. As noted above, the seven churches represent the Church in its entirety. The image of the seven lampstands is probably a reinterpretation of the golden lampstand with seven lights which stood in the temple, the menorah (see Ex 25:31 and Zech 4:2). The implication is that the Church, the followers of God and the Lamb, is the new, spiritual temple. Since John was writing probably after the destruction of the Jerusalem temple, it was especially important to understand how the presence of God might be felt in the new situation.

The description of the exalted Christ in verses 13-16 consists primarily of a number of allusions to passages in Daniel, Ezekiel, and other books of the Hebrew bible. John's artistry is apparent in the way all these disparate elements have been woven together to create a truly new and powerful whole. It is noteworthy that John does not use "Son of Man" as a title of Jesus, but speaks of *one like a son of man*, that is, one in human form, but who is more than human. Here John more accurately reflects the meaning of the phrase in Dan 7:13 than the Synoptic gospels do. Most striking is the way certain elements applied to Yahweh in the Hebrew bible are here applied to Christ: the *hair white as white wool, white as snow* (Dan 7:9), and the *voice like the sound of many waters* (Ezek 43:2). There is no systematic philosophical or theological reflection in the Apocalypse on the relationship between Jesus and God. What we do find is that some of the same images, symbols and functions are attributed to both interchangeably. For example, in 1:17 Jesus says *I am the first and the last* . . . . This attribute is very similar to those of God in 1:8 and 21:6. By using such images interchangeably, John does not necessarily imply anything about the metaphysical nature of Christ. The implications of such a procedure are functional—that Jesus mediates between human beings and God, that he is God's agent in both salvation and judgment.

As noted above, the seven messages of chapters 2 and 3 are part of the vision account which begins with 1:9. In the initial portion of the vision Christ is depicted as a transcendent overseer and judge. The seven messages have to do with the ordinary, daily lives of the individual churches. Exhortation about the concrete decisions facing the communities comes from the transcendent judge. The implication is that the smallest events of everyday life are of ultimate significance. Each decision, each action takes place under the all-seeing eye of the cosmic judge and thus takes on an importance of life and death.

The seven messages are very artfully related to their immediate context, the inaugural vision, and to the Apocalypse as a whole. They are also very skillfully related to one another in form and content. They all share a common pattern. Each message is introduced by Christ's command to John that he write. This element shows that the messages are placed in an apocalyptic framework. Revelation is an indirect and mysterious process. It is to be communicated in writing, no longer in direct speech. It is given, not directly to the believers, but from Christ to John, to the angel of each church and, only then, to the members of the community.

Each of the messages opens with the traditional formula of the prophetic messenger—"Thus says the Lord" or words to that effect. This formula expresses John's claim to speak on behalf of the risen Lord as an authentic prophet. Following the traditional, prophetic opening comes the body of the message. In each case, the body begins with the words "I know" followed by a characterization of the current situation of the community addressed. The body contains various prophetic words of admonition, praise, comfort and exhortation.

All seven messages end with the same two elements, though their order varies. One of these is the saying "He who has an ear, let him hear what the Spirit says to the churches." Other forms of this saying appear elsewhere in the Apocalypse (13:9) and in the gospels (for example, Mk 4:9 and Mt 11:15). Like the command which introduces each message, this saying reflects an apocalyptic view of reality. In the early church it was used to express the idea that the teaching of the prophets, and even of Jesus, was mysterious and could only be understood through special revelation. Here the saying shows that the messages are meant to be veiled and mysterious, but at the same time, they are addressed to all who have the Spirit, not just to the particular communities mentioned by name.

The other concluding element is the promise addressed to the one who conquers. In the context of the Apocalypse as a whole, "conquering" means being acquitted in a court of law. The acquittal of the faithful is paradoxical. It is expected that they will be found guilty in the local Roman courts and executed. But the testimony they give and their acceptance of death will win them the acquittal that counts—in the heavenly court, in the eyes of eternity.

MESSAGE TO THE LOYAL BUT UNLOVING CHURCH: EPHESUS. 2:1-7.

> **2** "To the angel of the church in Ephesus write: 'The words of him who holds the seven stars in his right hand, who walks among the seven golden lampstands.

[2]"'I know your works, your toil and your patient endurance, and how you cannot bear evil men but have tested those who call themselves apostles but are not, and found them to be false; [3]I know you are enduring patiently and bearing up for my name's sake, and you have not grown weary. [4]But I have this against you, that you have abandoned the love you had at first. [5]Remember then from what you have fallen, repent and do the works you did at first. If not, I will come to you and remove your lampstand from its place, unless you repent. [6]Yet this you have, you hate the works of the Nicolaitans, which I also hate. [7]He who has an ear, let him hear what the Spirit says to the churches. To him who conquers I will grant to eat of the tree of life, which is in the paradise of God.' "

An *angel* is associated with each of the seven churches. Many suggestions have been made about how this "angel" ought to be understood. Since "angel" refers to a heavenly being in the rest of the Apocalypse, it most likely does here also. The idea that each community has an angelic patron is probably a development from the Jewish idea that each nation had an angelic representative in heaven. Once again we meet the conviction that God is distant and that the earthly world is ordered by intermediary powers.

In the message to Ephesus, Christ is described as one *who walks among the seven golden lampstands*. This description calls to mind the vision of the one like a son of man (1:13) and reminds the readers that the message comes from the cosmic judge. It also prepares for the threat in 2:5—that if the faithful in Ephesus do not repent, their *lampstand* will be removed *from its place*. The threat is expressed in figurative language. It at least means that the church would lose its prominent position. It could mean more: that the church is in danger of having its relationship with Christ broken.

In the body of the message, the Ephesians are first praised (vss.2-3) and then admonished (vs.4). The references to the false *apostles* and to the *Nicolaitans* show that the local church is involved in controversy over authentic leadership and christian life. We will learn more about the Nicolaitans in the message to Pergamum. The community in Ephesus is praised for the stand it has taken on leadership, but their practice of christian love is not what it should be. The call for repentance (vs.5) is reinforced with the threat discussed above and with the promise to the one who conquers (vs.7).

The call for repentance implies that, even though one has been redeemed by Christ (see 1:5-6), salvation is not thereby guaranteed. One can still return the gift which has been given, still depart from the path. Apparently, life would be easier for the Ephesians if they rejected Christ, but they are *enduring patiently and bearing up* (vs.3).

It is noteworthy that the exhortation in this message, as in the others, is addressed more to the community than to individuals. This characteristic implies that christian life is a communal, social matter. Christian virtue has to do with shaping a community. It is not primarily a matter of individuals striving for perfection.

MESSAGE TO THE POOR AND PERSECUTED CHURCH: SMYRNA.
2:8-11.

> [8]"And to the angel of the church in Smyrna write: 'The words of the first and the last, who died and came to life.
> [9]"'I know your tribulation and your poverty (but you are rich) and the slander of those who say that they are Jews and are not, but are a synagogue of Satan. [10]Do not fear what you are about to suffer. Behold, the devil is about to throw some of you into prison, that you may be tested, and for ten days you will have tribulation. Be faithful unto death, and I will give you the crown of life. [11]He who has an ear, let him hear what the Spirit says to the churches. He who conquers shall not be hurt by the second death.'"

Christ as the author of this message is described as *the first and last, who died and came to life.* These words call to mind Christ's self-presentation to John near the beginning of the vision (1:17-18). These qualities are emphasized because the faithful in Smyrna are quite directly threatened with death. The life/death theme is picked up in the exhortation *Be faithful unto death, and I will give you the crown of life* (vs. 10) and by the promise that the one *who conquers shall not be hurt by the second death* (vs. 11).

Only the Roman governor had the power to administer capital punishment. But the attack on the Jews in the same context (vs. 9) is an indication that some Christians in Smyrna were probably accused before the Roman governor by Jews. According to Eusebius, Jewish citizens of Smyrna assisted the Roman authorities in convicting and executing some Christians in about 160, including the bishop, Polycarp. Thus, the statement that the Jews of Smyrna *are a synagogue of Satan* is a remark born out of strife and controversy. It is not an expression of anti-Semitism. The title "Jew" is respected; in fact, it is claimed for the followers of Christ.

In this message the universal problems of suffering and death are wrestled with. These experiences are given meaning here by presenting them as opportunities for the imitation of Christ. This story of Christ as the dying and rising savior has tremendous power to console. It implies that suffering and death are so deeply rooted in reality that even God's chosen one, the savior, had to suffer and die. Having so great a companion makes our own misfortunes easier to bear.

Also, suffering is presented in this message as a test (vs. 10). A positive side of misfortunes is that they provide opportunities to demonstrate and even to develop one's commitment, one's mettle. Hardship can help one see what is truly important and valuable. The testing of faith is like the refining of gold.

In the promise to the conqueror (vs. 11) we find ordinary death contrasted with *the second death.* This contrast implies that individual, physical death is not the greatest evil. In 20:14 we are told that the second death is eternal punishment in a lake of fire (see 20:10). In the message to Smyrna, this image expresses in a poetic way the conviction that apostasy is a greater evil than death.

MESSAGE TO THE ASSIMILATING CHURCH: PERGAMUM.
2:12-17

[12]"And to the angel of the church in Pergamum write: 'The words of him who has the sharp two-edged sword.

[13]"'I know where you dwell, where Satan's throne is; you hold fast my name and you did not deny my faith even in the days of Antipas my witness, my faithful one, who was killed among you, where Satan dwells. [14]But I have a few things against you: you have some there who hold the teaching of Balaam, who taught Balak to put a stumbling block before the sons of Israel, that they might eat food sacrificed to idols and practice immorality. [15]So you also have some who hold the teaching of the Nicolaitans. [16]Repent then, if not, I will come to you soon and war against them with the sword of my mouth. [17]He who has an ear, let him hear what the Spirit says to the churches. To him who conquers I will give some of the hidden manna, and I will give him a white stone, with a new name written on the stone which no one knows except him who receives it.'"

The message to Pergamum is similar to the one to Ephesus in several ways. As in the Ephesian message, the description of Christ calls to mind the opening vision of him as universal judge—he is the one *who has the sharp two-edge sword* (compare 2:12 with 1:16). Once again, the description is related to a threat. If the Pergamene Christians do not repent, Christ *will come* to them *soon* and make *war against* the Nicolaitans *with the sword of his mouth*. As in the message to the Ephesian church, the threat is figurative.

The faithful in Pergamum, like those in Ephesus, are first praised (vs.13) and then warned (vss.14-15). They are praised for avoiding apostasy even though one member of the church, *Antipas*, has been executed for refusing to deny his faith. They are criticized for harboring those *who hold the teaching of Balaam* and *of the Nicolaitans*.

The fidelity of the Pergamene Christians is especially praised because they live where *Satan's throne is*. The Roman seat of government of the province of Asia was located in Pergamum. In chapter 13, as we shall see, Satan is said to have given his authority to the Roman empire. So by Satan's throne the Roman seat of government is probably meant. Since the governor would normally reside there, Christians in Pergamum were especially vulnerable to accusation and arrest.

The references to *Balaam* and the *Nicolaitans* show that there was a controversy in Pergamum, as there was in Ephesus, over who the authoritative leaders were and what the authentic teaching on christian life was. There has been a good deal of controversy over who the leaders were who are being attacked in the messages and what their teaching was. As noted above, the saying *He who has an ear, let him hear. . .* implies that the messages are not straightforward descriptions of the situations in the various churches, but are purposely veiled and mysterious. Such certainly seems to be the case with the names *Balaam* and *Jezebel* (2:20), which are taken from the biblical tradition and used figuratively here. Since these are symbolic names, it is likely that *the Nicolaitans* is also.

One question that arises is how many different groups are involved. False teachers are mentioned in three of the messages: the Nicolaitans in the messages to the Ephesians (2:6) and to the Pergamenes (2:15), Balaam in the message to the Pergamenes (2:14), and Jezebel in the message to the church in Thyatira (2:20). All of these names seem to be associated with the same teaching. The word *so* (vs.15) implies that the teaching of the Nicolaitans and of Balaam is the same. The description of Balaam's teaching is the same as that of Jezebel. Both involve eating *food sacrificed to idols* and practicing *immorality*.

At first glance, it seems that these are issues related only to personal ethics. The word translated *practice immorality*, however, regularly has a double meaning in the Greek translation of the Jewish bible. Literally, it means sexual immorality, but it is regularly used as a metaphor for idolatry.

We know from Paul's first letter to the Corinthians that there was controversy in the early church on the issue of meat sacrificed to the pagan gods. In the first century much of the meat available in the markets and served in private homes and at banquets came from animals which had been slaughtered in a religious ceremony. Some Christians, like many Jews, refused to each such meat. One argument, apparently presupposed in the messages, against eating such meat is that it meant recognition or even worship of the pagan gods in question.

Therefore, the attacks on these false teachers reflect a controversy over what christian faith and community life are all about. It is a conflict over the basic issue of assimilation. The strict avoidance of meat sacrificed to idols would mean a separatist stance for the christian community. Such a stance would involve not only a radical critique of the religious life of the Roman empire, but a rejection of its social and economic life as well. The position advocated by the Nicolaitans would make possible participation in the social and economic life of the empire. However, it would open the door to syncretism and religious and ethical compromise as well.

So the call to repentance addressed to the Pergamenes (vs. 16) arises out of a theological critique of the contemporary culture. It is a polemic against misplaced and thoughtless reverence of the creature over the creator. It is a polemic against an unprincipled accommodation to the dominant cultural values.

MESSAGE TO THE COMPROMISING CHURCH: THYATIRA.
2:18-29.

[18]"And to the angel of the church in Thyatira write: 'The words of the Son of God, who has eyes like a flame of fire, and whose feet are like burnished bronze.

[19]"'I know your works, your love and faith and service and patient endurance, and that your latter works exceed the first. [20]But I have this against you, that you tolerate the woman Jezebel, who calls herself a prophetess and is teaching and beguiling my servants to practice immorality and to eat food sacrificed to idols. [21]I gave her time to repent, but she refuses to repent of her immorality. [22]Behold I will throw her on a sickbed, and those who commit adultery with her I will throw into great tribulation, unless they repent of her doings; [23]and I will strike her children dead. And all the churches shall know that I am he who searches mind and heart, and I will give to each of you as your works deserve. [24]But to the rest of you in Thyatira, who do not hold this teaching, who have not learned what some call the deep things of Satan, to you I say, I do not lay upon you any other burden; [23]only hold fast what you have, until I come. [26]He who conquers and who keeps my works until the end, I will give him power over the nations, [27]and he shall rule them with a rod of iron, as when earthen pots are broken in pieces, even as I myself have received power from my Father; [28]and I will give him the morning star. [29]He who has an ear, let him hear what the Spirit says to the churches.'"

The message to Thyatira is similar to those for Ephesus and Pergamum in form and content. The description of Christ refers once again to the vision of him as cosmic judge (compare 2:18 with 1:14-15). In the messages to Ephesus and Pergamum, the description was repeated in the body of the message in the form of a threat that Christ would indeed come to judge the community if they did not repent. This technique is not used in the message to Thyatira, but the description does seem to be related to the message in the same way implicitly. Mention of the *eyes like a flame of fire* and the *feet like burnished bronze* recall the opening vision of Christ as transcendent overseer and judge. In the body of the message, Christ threatens to judge the *woman Jezebel* by throwing her on a *sickbed, those who commit adultery with her* by throwing them *into great tribulation*, and *her children* by striking them *dead*. In vs. 23 we find a general description of Christ as judge; he is the one *who searches mind and heart* and who gives to each as one's works deserve.

The members of the church in Thyatira are, like those of Ephesus and Pergamum, first praised and then admonished. They are praised because their *works* of *love and faith and service* are increasing. In some ways, then, their practice of the christian way of life is sound. As we have already noted, the church in Thyatira was experiencing the same crisis in leaderhip with which those in Ephesus and Pergamum were struggling. Apparently, the church in Thyatira had been most deeply influenced by the assimilationist point of view. Not only did the community tolerate the teachers of compromise and accept their teaching, but some members had actually acted upon it (vss.20,22). The message rejects what is seen as unprincipled collaboration with Roman culture and religion and the people are called to repent.

The members of the church in Thyatira are praised for their *patient endurance* also. The Ephesians receive similar praise and their endurance is for the sake of Jesus' name (vs.3). Similar language is used in the message to Pergamum (vs. 13). There it becomes clear that *endurance* is the stance which the messages advocate in the face of persecution. It would seem then that some Christians in the city were compromising in order to avoid persecution, but others were remaining faithful.

The promise to the one who conquers makes use of imagery from one of the royal psalms (Ps 2:8-9)—*I will give him power over the nations, and he shall rule them with a*

rod of iron, as when earthen pots are broken in pieces . . . .
This image expresses vividly the fragile and transitory
character of political power and of the control by one
nation over others. The promise also involves the reversal
of the present situation: those who are powerless and persecuted now will rule in the future. The figurative language
shows that this should not be taken as a literal prediction of
a new regime similar in quality to all the old ones. Rather,
it is a symbolic expression of the conviction that the persecuted righteous actually are more powerful than the
unrighteous rulers—that, in spite of appearances, their
righteous lives and testimony have a deeper truth and a
deeper meaningfulness.

MESSAGE TO THE CHURCH WHICH HAS
FALLEN AWAY: SARDIS.
3:1-6.

3 "And to the angel of the church in Sardis write: 'The
words of him who has the seven spirits of God and the
seven stars.

"'I know your works; you have the name of being alive,
and you are dead. ²Awake, and strengthen what remains
and is on the point of death, for I have not found your
works perfect in the sight of my God. ³Remember then
what you received and heard; keep that, and repent. If
you will not awake, I will come like a thief, and you will
not know at what hour I will come upon you. ⁴Yet you
have still a few names in Sardis, people who have not
soiled their garments; and they shall walk with me in
white, for they are worthy. ⁵He who conquers shall be
clad thus in white garments, and I will not blot his name
out of the book of life; I will confess his name before
my Father and before his angels. ⁶He who has an ear, let
him hear what the Spirit says to the churches.'"

In the message to the church in Sardis, Christ is described
as one *who has the seven spirits of God and the seven stars.*
The seven spirits of God were said earlier to be before the

throne of God (1:4). Saying that Christ *has* these spirits implies that he now shares God's throne. The seven stars have been interpreted as the angels of the seven churches (1:20). They watch over the communities as Christ's agents. The theme of angels is taken up again in the promise to Sardis—Christ *will confess* the *name* of the one who conquers before God *and before his angels.* The idea being expressed is that the righteous lives of the faithful are part of what is lasting, what is ultimately real.

There is no praise for the community as a whole in Sardis. They are in grave danger, but all is not yet lost. The body of the message begins with the attempt to shock—*you are dead.* But what follows shows that *dead* is an exaggeration; they are only asleep but *on the point of death.* There is still time for repentance. This exhortation shows that as long as there is life, repentance is still possible, no matter how serious and lengthy the lapse.

Repentance involves starting over, returning to the basics and to the beginning. The Christians at Sardis are urged to *remember then what you received and heard,* that is, to recall the christian message as it is summarized and handed on from one believer to the next, from one community to another. Those who have fallen from christian faith and practice are asked to recall the basic proclamation and to open themselves once more to its power and claim on the hearer.

The exhortation to repentance is accompanied by a warning: *If you will not awake, I will come like a thief....* The image of Christ as a *thief* is rather startling here. In early christian exhortation, the *thief* is an image for the sudden and unexpected. Theft, as distinct from robbery, is by nature an event that catches the victim by surprise. So the point here is that the people of Sardis, like all others, *will not know at what hour* Christ will come upon them as judge.

This imagery belongs to the apocalyptic mentality which expects a sudden and violent end of the world. The messages can also speak of judging acts of Christ which do not imply the end of the world. Examples are his moving the lamp-stand of the Ephesian church from its place (2:5) and the threats issued against Jezebel and her followers (2:22-23). Warnings which imply an end of the world and those which do not both intend to influence the self-understanding and behavior of the readers in the present. The main point is that human beings are held accountable, regardless of when and how the accounting will take place.

A few members of the Church in Sardis are singled out for praise. They are *people who have not soiled their garments.* It is clear that the language here is symbolic. The image of clean or dirty garments symbolizing a person's inner condition is not unique to this passage. In Zechariah 3, Joshua the high priest is shown in a vision with filthy garments which symbolize his sin. God removes his iniquity and he is given clean clothes. In the early church baptism was practiced by immersion. The new Christian would lay aside his or her garments, be immersed nude in the baptimal waters, and then be clothed in white garments which symbolized her or his new spiritual life. It is likely that the *people who have not soiled their garments* are those who have not fallen from their baptismal purity.

The promise is given that these people will walk with Christ in white garments; they are numbered among the conquerors. The imagery of white garments is continued, but the symbolic meaning is different here. The white garments given to the conquerors symbolize glory and victory. The heavenly white garment expresses in a figura-tive way the idea that the faithful will have an existence like the angels after death. Here, as often in the Apocalypse, symbolism must be used when speaking of mysterious realities beyond what we can see, hear and touch in our everyday experience.

The final aspect of the promise is that the conqueror's name shall not be blotted *out of the book of life.* This is the first mention of the book of life, which appears several times in the Apocalypse (13:8; 17:8; 20:12,15; 21:27). Once again we meet a symbolic expression. The image involves a book kept in heaven in which the names of certain people are written. Originally, to have one's name in the book probably meant to be destined to survive some crisis with one's physical life intact (see, for example, Ex 32:32-33, Is 4:3). Later, "life" came to be used symbolically. Even when a person expected to die in a crisis, he or she could expect to gain "life" through that experience. Faithfulness and integrity are aspects of a life that transcends the physical.

MESSAGE TO THE WEAK AND FAITHFUL CHURCH: PHILADELPHIA.
3:7-13.

> [7]"And to the angel of the church in Philadelphia write: 'The words of the holy one, the true one, who has the key of David, who opens and no one shall shut, who shuts and no one opens.
>
> [8]"I know your works. Behold, I have set before you an open door, which no one is able to shut; I know that you have but little power, and yet you have kept my word and have not denied my name. [9]Behold, I will make those of the synagogue of Satan who say that they are Jews and are not, but lie—behold, I will make them come and bow down before your feet, and learn that I have loved you. [10]Because you have kept my word of patient endurance, I will keep you from the hour of trial which is coming on the whole world, to try those who dwell upon the earth. [11]I am coming soon; hold fast what you have, so that no one may seize your crown. [12]He who conquers, I will make him a pillar in the temple of my God; never shall he go out of it, and I will write on him the name of my God, and the name of the city of my God, the new Jerusalem which comes down from my God out of heaven, and my own new name. [13]He who has an ear, let him hear what the Spirit says to the churches.'"

The message to the church in Philadelphia is similar to the one addressed to Smyrna. Neither contains an attack on the teaching or practice of the church in question. Rather, they both emphasize exhortation and encouragement in the face of an impending crisis.

Christ as the author of the message to Philadelphia is described as the one *who has the key of David, who opens and no one shall shut, who shuts and no one opens*. The language used here is similar to that of Is 22:22. In that passage of Isaiah, a new steward is described who has full and exclusive authority over personal access to the king's presence. Applied here to Christ, this language implies that only he has the power to grant access to God; he is the only mediator.

The reference to a *key* also calls to mind one of the sayings of Christ in the opening vision—*I have the keys of Death and Hades* (1:18). Another saying from this verse, also dealing with the theme of life and death, was paraphrased in the message to Smyrna—*who died and came to life*. Like the church at Smyrna, the community at Philadelphia is threatened by persecution. So we would expect the theme of life and death to be prominent here also. In the context of the inaugural vision as a whole, the *key of David* corresponds to the *keys of Death and Hades*. Christ has power over death—he opens Death's door and frees from death. He also has power over life—he opens the door which leads to the presence of God. Being in the presence of God is true life.

In the body of the message Christ says *Behold, I have set before you an open door, which no one is able to shut*. Clearly the *open door* is a figurative expression. Some commentators interpret the image as a missionary opportunity, since "door" is used in that sense in 1 Cor 16:9 and elsewhere. But nothing else in the message to Philadelphia points clearly in that direction. In the gospel of John, Jesus is said to be the door of the sheep (10:7). There, the "door" refers to the means of salvation. Jesus is the mediator between the believers and eternal life, between them and God. This interpretation fits our passage also. It is Christ who has provided access to God for the faithful at Philadelphia. No one can cut them off from God.

This interpretation makes sense of the reference to the Jews which follows. The Jews in Philadelphia apparently disagreed with the Christians on their understanding of the role of Jesus. They challenged this understanding, but the Christians *kept* Jesus' *word and have not denied* his *name*. As in the message to Smyrna, controversy is reflected here over who are the legitimate Jews. Members of the local synagogue probably had expelled the Christians when they refused to change their minds about Jesus. Such expulsion would mean their loss of access to God. But they are reassured that the door remains open.

The members of the church in Philadelphia are said to be weak—they *have but little power*. This probably means that they have little political influence and social standing. Nevertheless, they have remained firm under persecution. Because of this faithfulness they receive a special promise, *I will keep you from the hour of trial which is coming on the whole world, to try those who dwell upon the earth*. The translation here is misleading. A better one would be *I will preserve you through the hour of trial . . . .* The next verse shows that the Philadelphians will continue to be tested just like all other dwellers upon the earth—they are told *hold fast what you have, so that no one may seize your crown*. Therefore, the promise is not that they will escape the time of trouble which is coming, but that they can face it confident of Christ's sustaining power.

The promise to the conquerors includes the words *I will make him a pillar in the temple of my God; never shall he go out of it*. We noted earlier that the Jerusalem temple was probably not standing any longer when the Apocalypse was written. In 1:20 the golden lampstand of the temple, the menorah, was reinterpreted. Now, the church is the lampstand in God's presence. Here, the pillars of the temple are reinterpreted. The pillars, those essential elements which bear the weight of the roof, are the conquerors, those who are faithful unto death.

MESSAGE TO THE CHURCH WHICH HAS BECOME COMPLACENT: LAODICEA. 3:14-22

[14]"And to the angel of the church in Laodicea write: 'The words of the Amen, the faithful and true witness, the beginning of God's creation.

[15]"'I know your works: you are neither cold nor hot. Would that you were cold or hot! [16]So, because you are lukewarm, and neither cold nor hot, I will spew you out of my mouth. [17]For you say, I am rich, I have prospered, and I need nothing; not knowing that you are wretched, pitiable, poor, blind, and naked. [18]Therefore I counsel you to buy from me gold refined by fire, that you may be rich, and white garments to clothe you and to keep the shame of your nakedness from being seen, and salve to anoint your eyes, that you may see. [19]Those whom I love, I reprove and chasten; so be zealous and repent. [20]Behold, I stand at the door and knock; if any one hears my voice and opens the door, I will come in to him and eat with him, and he with me. [21]He who conquers, I will grant him to sit with me on my throne, as I myself conquered and sat down with my Father on his throne. [22]He who has an ear, let him hear what the Spirit says to the churches.'"

The message to the church in Laodicea is closest in form to the message to Sardis. No praise is given to the church in Laodicea as a community. The description of Christ as author of the message repeats an element from the greeting, just as the description in the message to Sardis does. Here Christ is called *the faithful and true witness* (compare 1:5).

The church in Laodicea is condemned for being *lukewarm*. Christ threatens to vomit them out of his mouth. This message is harsher than the one to Sardis in that no individual members are singled out for praise. But even here the tone is hopeful. The Laodiceans are called to repentance as the nominal Christians of Sardis were.

In terms of the situation presupposed, this last message is similar to the one addressed to Thyatira. Some Christians in Thyatira apparently compromised their faith by mixing socially with influential, local non-Christians. Such mixing involved a religious syncretism as well, at least in externals. This behavior was probably related to a desire to succeed in business. This surmise fits in with what we know about Thyatira as a trading center with many guilds. Those members of the church in Thyatira who refused such compromise are praised for their patient endurance. "Endurance," as we have noted, refers to taking and holding a public stand which leads to disadvantage and even death.

The Laodicean Christians were rich and probably of high social standing in the city. Thus, they were under much less pressure to conform to pagan customs. Without such pressure, without a crisis, they became complacent. The message is intended to shake them out of their complacency. The description of Christ at the beginning already begins the process. Christ is the *faithful and true witness*. The implied question is what are the Laodiceans doing by way of witness. Christ is the *beginning of God's creation*. Have the Laodiceans relied so much on their wealth—created goods—that they have forgotten the creator? The implied exhortation is to remember that created goods are gifts which may be taken back at any time.

In the body of the message, the comfortable situation of the Christians in Laodicea is identified as *wretched, pitiable, poor, blind and naked*. They are living on the surface, a superficial life, without a sense of the deep struggle which is going on. They are counseled *to buy* from Christ *gold refined by fire*. In other words, they are called to bear witness to the truth, as Christ did, in the full knowledge that such testimony leads to suffering. But suffering is like a refiner's fire. The *nakedness* mentioned is life based only on material and transient things. The *white garments* and the *salve* symbolize the fruits of suffering in God's cause.

It is likely that the members of the church in Laodicea were aware of the arrests, trials, discrimination and even executions experienced by Christians in other cities. The message addressed to them implies that they counted themselves fortunate, even blessed by God, to have avoided such problems. But they are told *Those whom I love, I reprove and chasten.* Their peaceful existence is not a sign of God's favor, but of their own lack of zeal. This lack of zeal requires a change of heart (vs. 19).

Verse 20 contains a symbolic saying which has been interpreted in a variety of ways. The image of fellowship at a meal was commonly used in the early church to refer to the Kingdom of God, the final time of salvation. The primary meaning of the saying, therefore, is probably a call to be ready for the return of Christ at the end of days. Readiness for the Laodiceans implies a new zeal and willingness to bear witness. But since the saying is metaphorical, its meaning cannot be strictly limited to one such application. Its highly personal and individualistic language points the hearer to the many ways in which Christ makes his presence known. The Eucharist is one such way. For the wealthy Laodiceans, Christ could be recognized in the poor and powerless who might have knocked seeking their assistance.

No conclusion to John's inaugural vision is recorded. It simply ends with the announcement of the message to the Laodiceans, the seventh message of Christ, the universal judge and overseer. Immediately following is another vision which introduces the cycle of the seven seals.

C. JOHN SEES WHAT IS AND WHAT IS TO TAKE PLACE HEREAFTER.

4:1-8:5.

AS NOTED earlier, the Apocalypse is introduced in the prologue as a revelation of "what must soon take place" (1:1). When Christ appeared to John in his inaugural vision, he commissioned him, saying "write what you see, what is and what is to take place hereafter" (1:19). The seven messages, to a large extent, deal with "what is." They describe the current situations of the seven churches. But they also treat "what is to take place hereafter," in terms of both judgment and salvation. Some of the threats of judgment are conditional, like the threat that Christ might remove the lampstand of the Ephesians from its place (2:5). Others are predicted with certainty, but are individual and do not presuppose a general judgment, like the threats against Jezebel and her accomplices (2:22-23). But it is clear that the messages presuppose the return of Christ as judge of the whole world: Christ will come in an absolute sense near the "end" (2:25-26). The final time of the salvation of the faithful is presupposed by the promises to conquerors.

The fact that the threats and promises of the messages are addressed to particular local groups, or even at times to individuals, is due to the point of view of the messages. Although they presuppose imminent, cosmic judgment and salvation, their main concern is to point out to particular communities what meaning those cosmic events have for their lives in the here and now. It is assumed that the cosmic events will certainly happen. But communities and individuals can choose how those events will affect them. For that reason, many of the threats and promises are conditional.

Likewise, the cycle of visions related to the seven seals (4:1-8:5) describes both "what is" and "what is to take place hereafter." It is sometimes difficult to distinguish the two. Most would agree that the vision of the enthroned God in chapter 4 was intended to describe the present time of the prophet John. At the other extreme, most would consider the vision of judgment in 6:12-17 and the vision of salvation in 7:9-17 as future, from John's point of view at least.

The main difference between the seven messages and the seven seals is point of view. The messages describe judgment and salvation from the perspective of the seven churches. The seven seals describe the same events from the point of view of all humanity.

THE HEAVENLY COUNCIL.
4.

4 After this I looked, and lo, in heaven an open door! And the first voice, which I had heard speaking to me like a trumpet, said. "Come up hither, and I will show you what must take place after this." [2]At once I was in the Spirit, and lo, a throne stood in heaven, with one seated on the throne! [3]And he who sat there appeared like jasper and carnelian, and round the throne was a rainbow that looked like an emerald. [4]Round the throne were twenty-four thrones, and seated on the thrones were twenty-four elders, clad in white garments, with golden crowns upon their heads. [5]From the throne issue flashes of lightning, and voices and peals of thunder, and before the throne burn seven torches of fire, which are the seven spirits of God; ⁶and before the throne there is as it were a sea of glass, like crystal.

And round the throne, on each side of the throne, are four living creatures, full of eyes in front and behind: ⁷the first living creature like a lion, the second living creature like an ox, the third living creature with the face of a man, and the fourth living creature like a flying eagle. ⁸And the four living creatures, each of them with six wings, are full of eyes all round and within, and day and night they never cease to sing,

"Holy, holy, holy, is the Lord God Almighty,
  who was and is and is to come!"

⁹And whenever the living creatures give glory and honor and thanks to him who is seated on the throne, who lives for ever and ever, ¹⁰the twenty-four elders fall down before him who is seated on the throne and worship him who lives for ever and ever; they cast their crowns before the throne, singing,

¹¹"Worthy art thou, our Lord and God,
  to receive glory and honor and power,
  for thou didst create all things,
  and by thy will they existed and were created."

The remark *I looked* indicates the beginning of a new vision. John sees *an open door* in heaven. The phrase calls to mind the saying to the Philadelphians, "I have set before you an open door" (3:8). Its use here supports the interpretation given above. The *door* represents access to God. Here, John, as a prophet, is given a special kind of access. He is taken up to heaven *in the Spirit* and shown the divine throne and the heavenly council.

In chapter one, the vision of Christ is described as if it took place on earth. The vision of God in chapter 4 is related as if it took place in heaven. The difference in setting expresses a difference in the content of the visions. The vision of God and what follows belong to another "level" of reality. The latter visions deal with matters which are more mysterious, more hidden.

Like the description of Christ in 1:13-16, the vision of
the heavenly council in 4:1-11 is a powerful new vision,
made up in large part of motifs from well-known older
vision accounts. The idea that God is enthroned is a traditional element which appears in Ezek 1:28, Is 6:1 and
Dan 7:9. The *rainbow* around the throne and the *four
living creatures* are elements inspired by the great chariot
vision of Ezekiel 1-2. The atmosphere of worship in
general and the song of the living creatures (vs.8) in particular were inspired by Isaiah 6.

The presence of other thrones was probably inspired by
Dan 7:9. The scene in Dan 7:9-10 is a legal setting; the
ancient of days and those enthroned with him constitute
the heavenly court, sitting in judgment. There is no indication that ch. 4 of the Apocalypse describes a judicial
session. The presence of *elders* indicates that the scene
is a session of the heavenly "council."

There has been much debate over the identity of the
twenty-four elders. Various theories have been proposed,
some supposing them to be angels, others considering
them to be glorified human beings, and still others holding
them to be purely symbolic. The evidence in the Apocalypse
is simply not decisive. In any case, the term *elders* implies
that they are members of a heavenly council and thus are
companions and advisors of God, the king (see 15:3, where
God is given the title "king").

The idea that God is "king" of a "divine council" was
already traditional in John's time. The explicit mention of
elders, however, is probably related to the fact that many
social organizations of the time were ruled by councils
of elders—the Roman provinces of Asia Minor in co-
operation with the Roman governor, the synagogues, and
the local christian churches. This vision then is a good
example of the constant human endeavour to understand
the less known in terms of the familiar.

The *flashes of lightning* and the sounds *of thunder* are
traditional elements expressing the awesome character of
the divine presence. These motifs have their origin in the
experience of the majesty of the creator God in the storm,
which brings fertility to the land.

The *seven torches of fire* burning before the throne are the first hint of temple imagery in heaven as portrayed by the Apocalypse. Like the seven lampstands around Christ in 1:12-13, these seven torches call to mind the seven-branched lampstand which used to stand in the temple, the menorah. The presence of these torches enhances the majesty of the enthroned one and evokes a worshipful mood in the reader. The seven torches are interpreted as *the seven spirits of God.* As indicated earlier, these spirits should probably be understood as the seven archangels. In Jewish literature of the period, the archangels appear as God's agents in maintaining the natural order and in relating to humanity. Such agents were thought necessary because of the sense of a great gulf between the transcendent God and creation.

The *sea of glass, like crystal* is a very ancient element indeed. It is related to the praise of God as creator in vs.11. According to Gen 1:7, God made the firmament, the sky, and thereby separated the waters into those above and below the sky. In the Psalms, for example 93 and 104:3, we find evidence that this portion of the account of creation derives from an older creation story. In the older story, the creator God had to do battle with a sea monster before order could be established. So the "waters" are symbolic of chaos and destruction.

So the *sea* before the throne shows that the rule of God is always in tension with the opposing forces of disorder and disintegration. Creation did not bring about the extinction of these forces. They are still in existence, though held in check, even at the foot of the divine throne itself.

As noted above, the presence of the *seven torches* evokes the temple and a worshipful mood. This theme is further developed by the remark that *the four living creatures* praise God unceasingly by singing a hymn reminiscent of Is 6:3, *Holy, holy, holy . . . .* In Isaiah, the hymn goes on to say that "the whole earth is full of his glory." Such a statement would not fit in the Apocalypse, where the created world is so alienated from its creator that its destruction is necessary. Instead, the hymn concludes *who was and is and is to come.* This description of God occurred also in 1:8 and expresses a dynamic view of God. Although God is distant and gives little indication of involvement in the world at present, God's involvement does take place.

The theme of worship is continued in verses 9-11. In a striking symbolic gesture, the twenty-four elders *fall down before him who is seated on the throne* and *cast their crowns before the throne.* The implication is that all other rulers are subordinate to God and derive their power from God. If the heavenly elders acknowledge divine authority in that way, there is no room for earthly rulers who exercise their power complacently and assume their self-sufficiency.

Two reasons are given for worshipping God. God *lives for ever and ever.* No other being is associated with life so intensely and abundantly. The implication is that the transient ought not be worshiped; only the eternal is worthy of such honor.

The second reason for worshipping God is that all things were created by divine will. Again a contrast is implied. The creature should not be worshiped. The biblical tradition is full of warnings not to elevate the creature above the creator. At the same time it must be remembered that the creator can be known and loved only in and through particular created things and beings.

Two heavenly hymns are recorded in this chapter. With marvelous hyperbole it is announced that these songs are sung *day and night* without ceasing. The effect is a powerful scene of heavenly glory and reverence for the mysterious source of all being.

THE LAMB IS COMMISSIONED TO OPEN THE SCROLL.
5.

5 And I saw in the right hand of him who was seated on the throne a scroll written within and on the back, sealed with seven seals; ²and I saw a strong angel proclaiming with a loud voice, "Who is worthy to open the scroll and break its seals?" ³And no one in heaven or on earth or under the earth was able to open the scroll or to look into it, ⁴and I wept much that no one was found worthy to open the scroll or to look into it. ⁵Then one of the elders said to me, "Weep not; lo, the Lion of the tribe of Judah, the Root of David, has conquered, so that he can open the scroll and its seven seals." ⁶And between the throne and the four living creatures and among the elders, I saw a Lamb standing, as though it had been slain, with seven horns and with seven eyes, which are the seven spirits of God sent out into all the earth; ⁷and he went and took the scroll from the right hand of him who was seated on the throne. ⁸And when he had taken the scroll, the four living creatures and the twenty-four elders fell down before the Lamb, each holding a harp, and with golden bowls full of incense, which are the prayers of the saints; ⁹and they sang a new song, saying,

"Worthy art thou to take the scroll and to open its seals,
for thou wast slain and by thy blood didst ransom men
for God
from every tribe and tongue and people and nation,
¹⁰and hast made them a kingdom and priests to our God,
and they shall reign on earth."

¹¹Then I looked, and I heard around the throne and the living creatures and the elders the voice of many angels, numbering myriads of myriads and thousands of thousands, ¹²saying with a loud voice, "Worthy is the Lamb who was slain, to receive power and wealth and wisdom and might and honor and glory and blessing!" ¹³And I heard every creature in heaven and on earth and under the earth and in the sea, and all therein, saying, "To him who sits upon the throne and to the Lamb be blessing and honor and glory and might for ever and ever!" ¹⁴And the four living creatures said, "Amen!" and the elders fell down and worshiped.

The first four verses of chapter 5 imply that the heavenly council is faced with a serious problem. There is great need for someone to open the scroll with seven seals. Unfortunately, no one can be found who is able to perform this task. The strong angel invites volunteers without success. The tears of the prophet emphasize the quandary of the heavenly council as well as the desire of the faithful for the scroll to be opened.

At last a champion is found. He is described first of all in mighty images—*the Lion of the tribe of Judah, the Root of David,* the one who *has conquered.* The champion is acclaimed by thousands of *angels* and by *every creature in heaven and on earth and under the earth and in the sea.* The following visions (6:1-8:5) describe the exploits of the champion, the results of his opening the scroll.

In the context of the Apocalypse as a whole, it is clear that the problem facing the heavenly council is the rebellion of Satan which is paralleled by rebellion on earth. Chapter five presupposes the old story of Satan's rebellion against God which leads to the fall of creation. This old story is retold in the Apocalypse to express the feeling that the world had gone astray, that all creation was deeply alienated from the source of its being. Human relations had become unjust and the injustice had corrupted the natural world as well. The tears of the prophet express the desire of the faithful to have this situation rectified.

What solution is envisaged? The solution is linked to the scroll with seven seals. Many theories have been proposed about the nature and content of this scroll. The most likely is that the scroll with seven seals is a heavenly book of destiny in which future events are described. Such books appear in Jewish literature, for example, Dan 10:21. The existence of such books can be accepted by an apocalyptic mentality, because it is believed that the basic pattern of the events of the end has been predetermined by divine providence. This basic pattern is sometimes revealed by special favor to the visionaries.

In the Apocalypse, the events recorded in the scroll involve the defeat of Satan's rebellion, the judgment of the earth and the salvation of the faithful. In the old story, the champion is usually a young god who defeats the rebellious god in battle. That tradition is alluded to by the messianic titles *Lion of the tribe of Judah* and *Root of David*.

In some forms of the old story, the champion is wounded or even killed before he or his allies can finally defeat the opponent. That element of the old story is related in the Apocalypse to the death of Jesus, referred to by the symbol of the *Lamb*. In the new story of the Apocalypse, the death of the hero is seen as the first stage of his victory over the rebel. It is his sacrificial death which makes him worthy to set in motion the foreordained events of the end-time. The setting in motion of these events is symbolized by the opening of the scroll's seven seals.

Prior to chapter 5, the major symbol used for the risen Christ is the "one like a son of man" (1:13). As the one who commissions John and gives him the messages, this son of man is, in effect, in the role of revealer. It is, however, the function of judge which is emphasized in the context. It is one like a son of man who, according to Dan 7:13, comes with clouds (see Apoc 1:7). In the early church, this coming with clouds was associated with the role of cosmic judge. This role is alluded to repeatedly in the messages (2:5,16, 22-23; 3:3).

In chapter 5, the symbol of the *Lamb* is introduced, which is the dominant christological symbol of the Apocalpyse. It is probably related to the imagery of the lamb in the gospel of John. The relation is indirect, however, because a different Greek word is used. There is no clear evidence about the origin of the symbol. Many consider Isaiah 53 as the source of the image. In any case, it is clear that the death of Jesus is being interpreted symbolically, by analogy with the practice of sacrifice. In a theology of sacrifice, it is assumed that God chooses to remove the sin of a human being who offers an appropriate sacrifice to God in a worthy manner. With regard to the death of Jesus, the claim is that God has chosen to look upon his death as a fitting sacrifice which removes the sin of many *from every tribe and tongue and people and nation.*

The Lamb is said to have *seven horns.* The horn is traditionally an image for political or military power (see, for example, Dt 33:17). The image of a seven-horned lamb is obviously not a realistic one. The intent is to hint that the apparently helpless, slain lamb actually has great might. The *seven* horns imply that his power is complete, perfect.

Another unrealistic detail in the vision is the Lamb's *seven eyes.* The motif is also symbolic; the eyes stand for *the seven spirits of God sent out into all the earth.* This interpretation of the eyes calls to mind Zech 4:10, where the seven lamps are interpreted as "the eyes of the Lord, which range through the whole earth." In both passages, the idea is that the cosmic judge knows all that happens on the whole earth. In the Apocalypse, God knows all events through his agents, the seven archangels. It is striking in Apoc 5:6 that the seven eyes are attributed to the *Lamb,* while in Zechariah they are God's. This passage is one of many in the Apocalypse where the Lamb has the same function as God—in this case, as cosmic judge. It is through the story about Jesus the Christ that people perceive how God acts.

At several points in chapter 5, the Lamb is proclaimed *worthy—to take the scroll and to open its seals* (vs.9; see also vss.2 and 4) and *to receive power and wealth and wisdom and might and honor and glory and blessing* (vs.12). The idea expressed here centers on the scroll; since it is a heavenly book with awesome import, it is not accessible to just anyone. It is, in a sense, sacred. Only a person who has fulfilled certain requirements can approach it. A similar point is made in the message to the church in Sardis. Only those "who have not soiled their garments" are "worthy" to walk with Christ in white garments (3:4). In other words, only those who have fulfilled the requirement of remaining faithful will be allowed access to the full fellowship of Christ. In chapter 5, the Lamb is allowed access to the scroll because he *has conquered.* His "conquering" means that he has won a legal victory over Satan in the heavenly court through his testimony and death. This legal victory makes him *worthy* to overcome Satan by carrying out the sentence against him.

It is likely that for John this vision expressed what was already a present reality. Jesus had died and John understood his death as a conquest. The vision of chapter 5 is the Apocalypse's version of what other books of the New Testament call Jesus' resurrection or exaltation at the right hand of the Father. The death of Jesus has created a new situation, so the elders sing *a new song*. The death of Jesus is a cosmic turning point. It marks the beginning of the defeat of Satan. The forces of order and the creating power now manifest themselves through Jesus and his followers. This is why the Lamb is linked so closely to the one *who sits upon the throne* and why it is said that the followers of Jesus *shall reign on earth*.

THE BIRTH-PANGS OF THE NEW AGE: THE FIRST FOUR SEALS.
6:1-8.

> **6** Now I saw when the Lamb opened one of the seven seals, and I heard one of the four living creatures say, as with a voice of thunder, "Come!" [2] And I saw, and behold, a white horse, and its rider had a bow; and a crown was given to him, and he went out conquering and to conquer.
>
> [3] When he opened the second seal, I heard the second living creature say, "Come!" [4] And out came another horse, bright red; its rider was permitted to take peace from the earth, so that men should slay one another; and he was given a great sword.
>
> [5] When he opened the third seal, I heard the third living creature say, "Come!" And I saw, and behold, a black horse, and its rider had a balance in his hand; [6] and I heard what seemed to be a voice in the midst of the four living creatures saying, "A quart of wheat for a denarius, and three quarts of barley for a denarius; but do not harm oil and wine!"

[7]When he opened the fourth seal, I heard the voice of the fourth living creature say, "Come!" [8]And I saw, and behold, a pale horse, and its rider's name was Death, and Hades followed him; and they were given power over a fourth of the earth, to kill with sword and with famine and with pestilence and by wild beasts of the earth.

There has been much debate over the meaning of each of the first four seals and whether they refer to the past, present or future from John's point of view. Whether or not any of these visions has been fulfilled between John's time and our own has also been debated. As noted above, the vision of chapter 5 probably expresses John's view of the immediate past and the present. It is most likely that the first four seals and most of what follows refer to the future from John's point of view. Beginning with chapter 6, it is very difficult to link the visions of the Apocalypse with specific events and to discern a detailed chronological outline. In some visions, the original Greek text shifts from future to past to present in an apparently random fashion. These characteristics show that the Apocalypse should not be read as an orderly prediction of a series of events. Rather, it is a poetic vision which uses future language to express something about the nature of reality, to interpret the present.

As noted in the introduction to this commentary, the Apocalypse is an apocalyptic narrative in terms of its literary form. To put it another way, the Apocalypse is a story about the end of the world. A story is not critical history, but it has its own kind of truth. In the introduction, it was also noted that each cycle of visions tells the story of the end in its own way. The story of the opening of the scroll with seven seals is the whole story of the end. This story is told again in the cycle of the trumpets from another point of view. This repetition is somewhat like that of a musical theme and variations. Or, the Apocalypse may be compared to a trilogy of plays, all having the same characters and taking place at the same time. The formal difference between them is that they take place in different rooms of a house where all characters are staying. When you see the third play, you have the first two in mind and thus have a fuller understanding of all three. Yet, each can be seen independently.

From the point of view of content, the first four seals tell the story of the end in much the same way as the discourse attributed to Jesus in Mark 13 (see also Matthew 24 and Luke 21). Both accounts speak of war, famine and other forms of widespread tribulation. The form of the first four seals seems to have been inspired by two visions in the book of Zechariah (1:8-10 and 6:1-8). The first involves a man riding a red horse with red, sorrel and white horses nearby. The horses are those "whom the Lord has sent to patrol the earth." The other vision is of four chariots; each is drawn by horses of a different color—red, black, white and dappled gray. These chariots are also sent by God to patrol the earth.

Debate has been most intense over the meaning of the first seal—the *white horse* and *its rider*. It should never be forgotten that in the Apocalypse we are dealing with images and symbols. By their very nature, symbols have more than one meaning or application. Their ambiguity is one source of their powerful ability to speak to the human situation. It is sometimes possible to determine what John probably intended to express with a particular symbol. But there is no certain way of discovering his intention and, in any case, symbols and stories, once given shape, have lives of their own. So it is a mistake to try to reduce a symbol to one particular meaning or application.

In the case of the first seal, there are some hints which reveal what the primary intended meaning probably was. The main hint is the bow, which was the favorite weapon of the Parthian soldiers. Parthia was the major rival of Rome, a great power in the East, the successor to the Persian empire. In the first century, the Roman emperors were constantly worried about the possibility of a Parthian invasion. The allies of Rome also feared such an invasion. But some of the peoples who had been conquered by Rome looked forward to a Parthian victory which, they hoped, would free them from Rome's rule and lead to greater autonomy. Such sentiment was common in the eastern Mediterranean lands and many Jews shared it.

In light of that interpretation of the bow, the white horse symbolizes victory. A white horse was often ridden by the general celebrating a military victory in a triumphal march. The crown was sometimes given as a military decoration or as a prize for public service in war. In a later cycle of visions, it becomes apparent that John expected Rome to be destroyed by an invasion of the Parthian and other eastern armies. It is not surprising that the vision of the first seal makes a rather positive, even joyful, impression. Since John believes Rome to be a tool of Satan, its downfall would be victory for the forces of good.

The placement of this vision at the beginning of the cycle of the seals shows that John viewed the imminent fall of Rome as the beginning of the end. Even though Rome did not fall as soon as John expected or in the way this vision suggested, it still expresses a powerful truth. The power of any great nation is limited. A certain scope is granted, a certain length of time. The awareness of these limitations is symbolized by the rider on the white horse.

When the *second seal* is opened, *out came another horse, bright red.* The symbolism in this vision is clear, though general. In association with the *great sword*, the red horse symbolizes bloodshed. Usually, the red horse is associated with war, but the text is not that specific. Its rider *was permitted to take peace from the earth, so that men should slay one another.* The imagery would fit international war, widespread outbreaks of civil war or a general breakdown of social order accompanied by frequent murders. In any case, the vision is a terrifying picture of the breakdown of order and the threat of violent death.

The opening of the *third seal* evokes the appearance of *a black horse.* Its rider carries *a balance in his hand.* The significance of the balance is interpreted by *a voice.* The *denarius* was the daily wage of the working man of the time. Usually, a denarius could buy eight to sixteen times more wheat and eight times more barley than the amounts mentioned. So bread, the main staple, would be very scarce. At the same time, oil and wine, which were luxuries, would be plentiful. These conditions seem to be a visionary heightening of the actual conditions under the emperor Domitian, the period during which the Apocalypse was probably written. The great landowners were reluctant to raise grain because olives and vineyards were more profitable. So John depicts one of the woes near the end as a time when the wealthy prosper and the ordinary person must go hungry.

The scene which follows the opening of the *fourth seal* rivals that following the second in its gruesome character. The *horse* which appears is *pale*—the pallid color of death. Its rider is *Death* himself; the same Greek word can mean *pestilence* or plague (see vs.8). His companion is Hades, the ruler of the underworld. Sometimes Hades is described as the personified realm of the dead with a huge mouth which swallows up all the living beings within reach.

The symbolism is general, like that of the second seal, and cannot be limited to any specific historical events. One-fourth of all humanity are allowed to die, are given over into the hands of Death and Hades. It is not yet the end—there is a limit to the number who die. At the same time, the number is so large that the survivors must live in great fear and mourning. The means of death are varied; *sword* and *famine* refer to the second and third seals and symbolize hardships created by human beings for others. *Pestilence* and *wild beasts* are new elements. They symbolize the hostility of nature.

The first four seals should not be read as predictions of events which will follow logically one upon the other. Each portrays one aspect of a time of woe, a time in which all humanity will suffer. In the context of the Apocalypse as a whole, this time of woe is interpreted as the birth-pangs of a new age, a new creation. All suffer, apparently indiscriminately. But, in reality, the suffering is providential. It is testing for some, punishment for others. The next two visions reveal this hidden truth.

THE VISION OF THE SOULS UNDER THE ALTAR: THE FIFTH SEAL.
6:9-11

> [9]When he opened the fifth seal, I saw under the altar the souls of those who had been slain for the word of God and for the witness they had borne; [10]they cried out with a loud voice, "O Sovereign Lord, holy and true, how long before thou wilt judge and avenge our blood on those who dwell upon the earth?" [11]Then they were each given a white robe and told to rest a little longer, until the number of their fellow servants and their brethren should be complete, who were to be killed as they themselves had been.

The souls of those who had been slain are portrayed as *under the altar.* This is the first mention of an altar in the Apocalypse. The vision of the enthroned one in chapter 4 evoked the atmosphere of the temple. The image of a heavenly temple is explicit elsewhere in the book (14:17). The portrayal of the souls under the altar implies that their deaths were sacrifices to God.

Even though their deaths are interpreted as sacrifices, justice requires that innocent blood be avenged. The souls cry out to demand this justice. The response presupposes the apocalyptic tradition that a predetermined, fixed number of souls must go to their resting place before the end could arrive. The Apocalypse gives that tradition a new twist. The traditional idea was that, when the underworld is full of souls, it will give them up for the general judgment, just as the womb pushes out the child when it has fully distended. According to this passage, the key is not simply how many people have passed on, but how many have been *killed* as the souls under the altar had been—*for the word of God and for the witness they had borne.* When the foreordained number has been reached, the end would come. This idea means that the woes of the end-time are understood as punishment on those who have shed innocent blood. It also means that the suffering of the faithful is not in vain. The death of each martyr brings the end closer and thus helps bring about the new age.

This vision expresses the conviction that suffering is not random, not meaningless. There is a cosmic plan, there is divine providence. Those who keep God's word and witness to the truth need not fear death. They can rejoice in the knowledge that their suffering contributes to the manifestation of God's rule.

THE DAY OF WRATH:
THE SIXTH SEAL.
6:12-17.

> [12]When he opened the sixth seal, I looked, and behold, there was a great earthquake; and the sun became black as sackcloth, the full moon became like blood, [13]and the stars of the sky fell to the earth as the fig tree sheds its winter fruit when shaken by a gale; [14]the sky vanished like a scroll that is rolled up, and every mountain and island was removed from its place. [15]Then the kings of the earth and the great men and the generals and the rich and the strong, and every one, slave and free, hid in the caves and among the rocks of the mountains, [16]calling to the mountains and rocks, "Fall on us and hide us from the face of him who is seated on the throne, and from the wrath of the Lamb; [17]for the great day of their wrath has come, and who can stand before it?"

As noted earlier, each cycle of visions in the Apocalypse tells the whole story of the end of the world. Each repeats the basic pattern of persecution, judgment and salvation. In the fifth seal, the vision of the souls under the altar. The sixth seal is a vision of judgment.

This vision describes *the great day* of the *wrath* of the enthroned one and of the Lamb. It begins with a powerful description of cosmic collapse. Both earth and heaven are devasted. The devastation is portrayed in vivid, poetic images. The images are traditional and express the idea that the creator has a destructive face also.

All people are affected, but some are singled out—*the kings of the earth and the great men and the generals and the rich and the strong*. The placement of this vision immediately following the souls' cry for justice implies that the day of wrath is the vengeance for which they prayed. The woes of the end are punishment for the rich and mighty who abused their power.

This vivid portrayal of judgment expresses the conviction that wealth and power carry heavy responsibility, that those who abuse them are held accountable. Also, it reminds us all of the fragility of human accomplishment in comparison with the mysteries of the cosmos.

THE SALVATION OF THE FAITHFUL: AN INTERLUDE.
7

7   After this I saw four angels standing at the four corners of the earth, holding back the four winds of the earth, that no wind might blow on earth or sea or against any tree. ²Then I saw another angel ascend from the rising of the sun, with the seal of the living God, and he called with a loud voice to the four angels who had been given power to harm earth and sea, ³saying, "Do not harm the earth or the sea or the trees, till we have sealed the servants of our God upon their foreheads." ⁴And I heard the number of the sealed, a hundred and forty-four thousand sealed, out of every tribe of the sons of Israel, ⁵twelve thousand sealed out of the tribe of Judah, twelve thousand of the tribe of Reuben, twelve thousand of the tribe of Gad, ⁶twelve thousand of the tribe of Asher, twelve thousand of the tribe of Naphtali, twelve thousand of the tribe of Manasseh, ⁷twelve thousand of the tribe of Simeon, twelve thousand of the tribe of Levi, twelve thousand of the tribe of Issachar, ⁸twelve thousand of the tribe of Zebulun, twelve thousand of the tribe of Joseph, twelve thousand sealed out of the tribe of Benjamin.

⁹After this I looked, and behold, a great multitude which no man could number, from every nation, from all tribes and peoples and tongues, standing before the throne and before the Lamb, clothed in white robes, with palm branches in their hands, ¹⁰and crying out with a loud voice, "Salvation belongs to our God who sits upon the throne, and to the Lamb!" ¹¹And all the angels stood round the throne and round the elders and the four living creatures, and they fell on their faces before the throne and worshiped God, ¹²saying, "Amen! Blessing and glory and wisdom and thanksgiving and honor and power and might be to our God for ever and ever! Amen."

¹³Then one of the elders addressed me, saying, "Who are these, clothed in white robes, and whence have they come?" ¹⁴I said to him, "Sir, you know." And he said to me, "These are they who have come out of the great tribulation; they have washed their robes and made them white in the blood of the Lamb.

¹⁵Therefore are they before the
throne of God,
and serve him day and night
within his temple;
and he who sits upon the throne
will shelter them with his presence.
¹⁶They shall hunger no more, neither
thirst any more;
the sun shall not strike them, nor
any scorching heat.
¹⁷For the Lamb in the midst of the
throne will be their shepherd,
and he will guide them to springs
of living water;
and God will wipe away every tear
from their eyes."

The vision of the Day of Wrath is followed by two vision accounts (7:1-8 and 9-17) which are not linked to one of the seven seals. Rather, they form a kind of interlude between the sixth and the seventh seals. Their lack of association with one of the seals makes them stand out, gives them a certain emphasis. Both of these visions portray the third element of the pattern repeated in each cycle—the salvation of the faithful. The second vision (7:9-17) does so more clearly and dramatically and thus is the climax of the cycle of the seals.

The first vision (7:1-8) opens with the portrayal of *four angels standing at the four corners of the earth, holding back the four winds of the earth*. The setting is cosmic—the whole earth is in view. The association of four angels with four winds is part of the current view of God and the natural world. God, the creator, indeed controls nature, but not directly. The divine will is carried out by intermediary beings. This idea preserves the transcendence of God, yet maintains the conviction that the world is under God's control.

The four winds here are agents of divine punishment, as they are in Jer 49:36. The angels are told to wait for the faithful to be sealed before unleashing the winds against the earth and sea. The dramatic effect is striking—a suspenseful stillness; even the leaves on the trees are motionless.

Next, John sees *another angel* ascending *from the rising of the sun*, that is, from the East. This angel is about to direct the sealing of *the servants of our God upon their foreheads*. This powerful image was inspired by Ezekiel 9. In that vision of Ezekiel, those who mourn the abuse of the temple cult are marked on the foreheads by an angel just before the inhabitants of Jerusalem are slaughtered by avenging angels. The image is mentioned again in Apoc 9:4. Those who are sealed will not be harmed by the plague of locusts.

Many commentators have remarked that there is no indication that the faithful are preserved from the woes brought about by the first six seals. They have wondered why the sealing comes so late. Some have even suggested that this vision account is out of place, that originally it was before 6:12 or even 6:1. Once again, we have the problem of modern commentators demanding too much of the wrong kind of logic from the Apocalypse. Perhaps, as 9:4 indicates, the sealing was supposed to protect the faithful from certain demonic plagues. We would then have an element from the second version of the story appearing somewhat out of context in the first story, the cycle of the seals. But it is clear from the messages that at least some of the faithful are expected to be killed in persecution. So the image of sealing does not have the same meaning in the Apocalypse that it had in Ezekiel. It does not symbolize divine protection from physical harm and death. Rather, it symbolizes divine protection within and in spite of suffering and death.

Then John *heard the number of the sealed, a hundred and forty-four thousand sealed, out of every tribe of the sons of Israel* . . . . Because of the mention of the twelve tribes, one by one, in the following verses, some commentators have thought that the 144,000 are Jews or Jewish-Christians, and that the multitude in the next vision are gentile Christians. It is unlikely that John intended such a distinction, since, in the messages, the title "Jews" is denied the members of the synagogue. By implication, it is the followers of Jesus who are the true *sons of Israel.*

A more difficult question is whether the 144,000 symbolize all the faithful or a particular group within the faithful. A group of 144,000 appears in a later vision with the Lamb on Mount Zion (14:1-5). It is likely that both visions refer to the same group. In 14:1-5 the 144,000 do not seem to represent all the faithful, but a special group within the faithful. We will see what defines the group when we discuss the vision in 14:1-5.

The *tribe of Judah* is mentioned first because it is the tribe from which Jesus, the Messiah, came (see 5:5). The *tribe of Manasseh* is mentioned even though Manasseh is included in *Joseph.* At the same time, Dan is omitted. The reason for the omission of Dan is a tradition that the Anti-Christ would come forth from that tribe. So Manasseh is added to make up the number twelve.

The second vision (7:9-17) portrays *a great multitude which no man could number, from every nation ... standing before the throne . . . clothed in white robes.* One of the elders tells John that they are those *who have come out of the great tribulation; they have washed their robes ... in the blood of the Lamb.* This is a vision of the ultimate, complete salvation and triumph of all the faithful. The vision of the multitude in white robes symbolizes the glory and joy of the faithful in the new age. Salvation involves enjoying the presence of God and the Lamb (vvs.9,15). The *palm branches* recall celebrations of victory and joy following a war. The faithful join in the heavenly liturgy and worship by praising the ones who have delivered them (vs.10).

It is sometimes assumed that all in this great multitude have died for their faith. The vision does not clearly imply such a universal martyrdom. It was certainly expected that for some, "endurance" would include death (see 2:10,13). But it would not necessarily be required of all. Note that their robes are white because they have been washed in the blood of the Lamb. This imagery refers to the traditional understanding of Jesus' death as a vicarious sacrifice. It does not of itself imply the expectation that all the faithful will perish in persecution.

The vision closes with a beautiful hymn expressing the nature of salvation through various metaphors. Hunger and thirst will be satisfied. The fulfillment of these physical needs points beyond itself to the fulfillment of less tangible kinds of hunger and thirst—for knowledge, for justice, for love. The faithful will be preserved from *scorching heat* and will be guided to *springs of living water.* Excessive heat, which brings sterility to the land and lethargy to humanity, will be no more. Water will be abundant. These images express abundant and fertile life. Finally, *God will wipe away every tear from their eyes.* The image of a parent's tender concern for a crying child is used as the ultimate image of salvation.

SILENCE, SMOKE AND FIRE: THE SEVENTH SEAL.
8:1-5.

> **8** When the Lamb opened the seventh seal, there was silence in heaven for about half an hour. [2]Then I saw the seven angels who stand before God, and seven trumpets were given to them. [3]And another angel came and stood at the altar with a golden censer; and he was given much incense to mingle with the prayers of all the saints upon the golden altar before the throne; [4]and the smoke of the incense rose with the prayers of the saints from the hand of the angel before God. [5]Then the angel took the censer and filled it with fire from the altar and threw it on the earth; and there were peals of thunder, loud noises, flashes of lightning, and an earthquake.

The immediate result of the opening of the seventh seal is *silence in heaven for about half an hour*. The silence is a powerful image, and, as usual, there has been debate about its significance. One suggestion is that the silence is necessary so that *the prayers of all the saints* can be heard in heaven. But no mention is made of the prayers being "heard." In any case, the application of earthly rules to a heavenly scene is out of place. Another suggestion is that the silence symbolizes the return to primeval silence following the destruction of the old heaven and earth. Such an idea is expressed in 2 Esdr 7:30. But there the silence is to last seven days—a number symbolizing completeness. Here the silence lasts half an hour, an incomplete number. The most likely interpretation is that the silence is mentioned purely for dramatic effect. The length of the silence fits this function—an uneven portion of time which builds suspense for what is to happen next.

The opening of the last seal has two further results: the appearance of *the seven angels who stand before God* who are given *seven trumpets* and the coming of *another angel* standing *at the altar with a golden censer.* Since the appearance of the angels with the trumpets results from the opening of the seventh seal, the whole cycle of the trumpets is, in a sense, a series of events set in motion by the opening of the seventh seal. But this relationship should not be understood chronologically. We have already noted that the whole story of the end is told in the cycle of the seven seals. So the interlocking of the two cycles is a literary device. It provides an opportunity for beginning again and telling the story from another perspective.

The vision of the angel with *a golden censer* (vss.3-5) is a pivotal vision which helps to link the cycle of the seals with the cycle of the trumpets. The angel *stood at the altar.* This allusion to the heavenly altar brings to mind the vision of the souls under the altar which followed the fifth seal (6:9-11). In the transitional vision (8:3-5), the angel offers incense along with *the prayers of all the saints.* The mention of prayers also calls to mind the fifth seal with its cry of the slain for justice.

At the same time this vision prepares the way for the seven trumpets. The angel filled the censer with *fire from the altar and threw it on the earth.* This act is followed by thunder, lightning and an earthquake—phenomena which express the mighty presence of God. The implication is that God is about to visit the earth in judgment.

In this interlocking vision, the offering of the prayers of the saints is followed by the symbolic act of casting fire upon the earth. The implication is that the plagues which follow the seven trumpets are divine acts of judgment executed as vengeance for the suffering of the faithful.

D. PLAGUES PREPARE THE WAY FOR THE KINGDOM OF GOD. 8:6 - 11:19.

WE NOTED EARLIER that the seven messages look forward to judgment and salvation from the point of view of particular christian communities. The seven seals describe the events of judgment and salvation from the perspective of all humanity. The cycle of the seven trumpets tells the same story, this time from a cosmic point of view. With each retelling, the story's universal implications become more apparent. John begins with the individual as part of a particular christian community and ends this first half of the Apocalypse with visions involving all creation.

Since the trumpets are introducing basically the same story told by the seals, it is inappropriate to relate the two cycles to one another chronologically. The story of the seals is veiled and fragmentary. This second cycle has those qualities too, but seems to reveal a little more fully John's vision of the end. This fuller revelation has two aspects. As noted above, the involvement of the natural world is greater in the trumpets. The other aspect concerns the magnitude of the crisis. In the fourth seal, one quarter of all humanity is destined to die in the time of woe. According to the sixth trumpet, the number will be one third.

Once again, it must be kept in mind that the Apocalypse uses images and symbols to tell a story of the end. The point is not to provide the readers with a timetable for the future, but to give them an understanding of reality to interpret and shape their present lives.

THE PURGING OF THE EARTH:
THE FIRST FOUR TRUMPETS.
8:6-13.

[6]Now the seven angels who had the seven trumpets made ready to blow them.

[7]The first angel blew his trumpet, and there followed hail and fire, mixed with blood, which fell on the earth; and a third of the earth was burnt up, and a third of the trees were burnt up, and all green grass was burnt up.

[8]The second angel blew his trumpet, and something like a great mountain, burning with fire, was thrown into the sea; [9]and a third of the sea became blood, a third of the living creatures in the sea died, and a third of the ships were destroyed.

[10]The third angel blew his trumpet, and a great star fell from heaven, blazing like a torch, and it fell on a third of the rivers and on the fountains of water. [11]The name of the star is Wormwood. A third of the waters became wormwood, and many men died of the water, because it was made bitter.

[12]The fourth angel blew his trumpet, and a third of the sun was struck, and a third of the moon, and a third of the stars, so that a third of their light was darkened; a third of the day was kept from shining, and likewise a third of the night.

[13]Then I looked, and I heard an eagle crying with a loud voice, as it flew in midheaven, "Woe, woe, woe to those who dwell on the earth, at the blasts of the other trumpets which the three angels are about to blow!"

The form of the cycle of the trumpets was inspired by the image of the trumpet blast on the Day of the Lord (see Joel

2:1 and Is 27:13). The content seems to be a free adaptation of the ten plagues against the Egyptians which preceded the exodus (Exodus 7-10). The story of the exodus is being used as a model for understanding the situation in which John's first readers found themselves. An analogy is seen between their ill treatment by the Romans and the slavery experienced by the children of Israel in Egypt. Just as God delivered his people in the past, so will he again.

The *seven angels* are the seven spirits who stand before the heavenly throne (8:2, 1:4). In 5:6 they are the "seven eyes" of the Lamb and are sent out into all the earth. These, as we have noted before, are probably the seven archangels of Jewish tradition, who were mediators between God and creation. The image "eyes" implies that they report to God what happens on earth. Here, they carry out the punishments due for the transgressions they have reported.

The *first trumpet* unleashes *hail and fire, mixed with blood*; a third of the earth is affected. This disaster is reminiscent of the seventh plague against the Egyptians (Ex 9:13-26). The *second trumpet* causes *a third of the sea* to become *blood*. This second catastrophe calls to mind the first Egyptian plague, when the Nile was turned into blood (Ex 7:14-24). The *third* and *fourth trumpets* have no direct parallels in the exodus story.

The plagues in the exodus story were directed against the land, crops, animals and people of Egypt. Here, the entire world is affected in each of its traditional four aspects —the earth (first trumpet), the sea (second trumpet), the fresh waters (third trumpet), and the heavenly bodies (fourth trumpet). The exodus story concerns the experiences of Israel as a people. The Apocalypse focuses on the trials of the faithful, but it has a more universal scope. The sufferings of the followers of Jesus are seen as one symptom of the corruption and alienation of the entire cosmos. The partial destruction of the world in these four trumpets foreshadows the account of total destruction in the last cycle of visions in the Apocalypse.

The expectation of the destruction of the world expresses a profound alienation from the world as experienced. It is no longer a manifestation of the work and presence of the creator. The logic of the story is that human sin corrupts nature. There is a deep solidarity between human action and the state of the natural world. If humanity is sinful and unrepentant, they contaminate the natural elements by their evil deeds. Then not only must people be punished, but the cosmos must be destroyed also.

After the fourth trumpet is sounded *an eagle* appears *in midheaven*, crying out a saying of doom. The saying characterizes the last three trumpets as three woes.

THE BOTTOMLESS PIT IS OPENED:
THE FIFTH TRUMPET.
9:1-12.

> **9** And the fifth angel blew his trumpet, and I saw a star fallen from heaven to earth, and he was given the key of the shaft of the bottomless pit; ²he opened the shaft of the bottomless pit, and from the shaft rose smoke like the smoke of a great furnace, and the sun and the air were darkened with the smoke from the shaft. ³Then from the smoke came locusts on the earth, and they were given power like the power of scorpions of the earth; ⁴they were told not to harm the grass of the earth or any green growth or any tree, but only those of mankind who have not the seal of God upon their foreheads; ⁵they were allowed to torture them for five months, but not to kill them, and their torture was like the torture of a scorpion, when it stings a man. ⁶And in those days men will seek death and will not find it; they will long to die, and death will fly from them.
>
> ⁷In appearance the locusts were like horses arrayed for battle; on their heads were what looked like crowns of gold; their faces were like human faces, ⁸their hair like women's hair, and their teeth like lions' teeth; ⁹they

had scales like iron breastplates, and the noise of their wings was like the noise of many chariots with horses rushing into battle. [10]They have tails like scorpions, and stings, and their power of hurting men for five months lies in their tails. [11]They have as king over them the angel of the bottomless pit; his name in Hebrew is Abaddon, and in Greek he is called Apollyon.

[12]The first woe has passed; behold, two woes are still to come.

When *the fifth angel blew his trumpet*, John saw *a star fallen from heaven to earth*. In the ancient world, stars were not thought of as great bodies of gases, as they are today. Rather, they were usually considered divine beings. Among Jews, the stars were identified with angels. The star falling from heaven to earth evokes the story of the fall of Satan, one of the most glorious angels ("Lucifer"). This story was originally about a Canaanite god and was applied to the king of Babylon in Isaiah 14. The story of the fall of Satan is often told to explain the origin of evil in the world.

The ancient Jews had other stories which dealt with the same problem. In one, a whole order of angels left heaven, came down to earth, and taught humanity all sorts of evil. The agents of God, loyal angels, subdued the rebellion temporarily by imprisoning the fallen angels in a pit. In this vision, the fallen sar or angel is *given the key of the shaft of the bottomless pit* and opens it. This vision seems to be an adaptation of the story of the fallen angels. In primordial time, it implies, the wicked angels were imprisoned in a pit and evil was temporarily controlled. But now there is a resurgence of evil, things are even worse than before, because the evil spirits have been released from their confinement and set loose upon the earth.

This traditional story of the origin of evil is combined here with the account of the eighth plague against the Egyptians, the plague of locusts (Exodus 10). That part of the exodus story had already been reinterpreted by the prophet Joel. In the book of Exodus, a swarm of locusts was God's instrument in chastising the enemies of God's people. In Joel 2, a plague of locusts is about to be used by the Lord to punish the Lord's own people.

As in the first four trumpets, the image from Exodus is intensified and universalized. The locusts are not the ordinary, though formidable, kind which consume plants. Rather, they are *given power like the power of scorpions of the earth* and they torture human beings with stings so painful that one longs for death. Their activity is not limited to one region, but they attack all people who are not sealed with the seal of the living God.

In the last part of the vision account, military imagery is used in connection with the locusts, as it was in Joel 2. The locusts appear as *horses arrayed for battle,* they have *scales like iron breastplates, and the noise of their wings was like the noise of many chariots with horses rushing into battle.* The military imagery is reinforced by the human characteristics of the locusts—the gold crowns would lead the reader to think of kings from the East; they have human faces and hair. This aspect of the imagery would evoke the tradition that the end time would be a time of war and perhaps recall the first seal with its allusion to the Parthians.

All of the imagery of the vision is intended to create an impression of the rampant resurgence of chaos and evil during the end time. The emphasis on this aspect of the end time probably reflects John's evaluation of the civilization of his day. The symbolic character of the vision is indicated by the return to imagery from the old story of angelic rebellion. The leader of these hostile creatures is *the angel of the bottomless pit.* His Hebrew name means "destruction"; the Greek, "destroyer."

This outbreak of evil is the *first woe.*

CAVALRY FROM THE EUPHRATES: THE SIXTH TRUMPET.
9:13-21.

> [13]Then the sixth angel blew his trumpet, and I heard a voice from the four horns of the golden altar before God, [14]saying to the sixth angel who had the trumpet,

"Release the four angels who are bound at the great river Euphrates." [15]So the four angels were released, who had been held ready for the hour, the day, the month, and the year, to kill a third of mankind. [16]The number of the troops of cavalry was twice ten thousand times ten thousand; I heard their number. [17]And this was how I saw the horses in my vision; the riders wore breastplates the color of fire and of sapphire and of sulphur, and the heads of the horses were like lions' heads, and fire and smoke and sulphur issued from their mouths. [18]By these three plagues a third of mankind was killed, by the fire and smoke and sulphur issuing from their mouths. [19]For the power of the horses is in their mouths and in their tails; their tails are like serpents, with heads, and by means of them they wound.

[20]The rest of mankind, who were not killed by these plagues, did not repent of the works of their hands nor give up worshiping demons and idols of gold and silver and bronze and stone and wood, which cannot either see or hear or walk; [21]nor did they repent of their murders or their sorceries or their immorality or their thefts.

When *the sixth angel blew his trumpet*, John heard a voice from the same altar mentioned in the pivotal vision between the seals and the trumpets (8:3-5). The voice gives a command which unleashes new plagues. The reference to the altar reinforces the impression that these plagues are presented as punishment for the wrongs against the faithful.

The command issued by the voice is that *the four angels who are bound at the great river Euphrates* be released. The mention of the Euphrates calls the great empires of the East to mind, in John's time, the Parthians. This alusion is reinforced by mention of the *number of the troops of cavalry, the horses,* their *riders* and the *breastplates* worn by the riders. This aspect of the vision evokes the impression of a great battle in the end time, the same one alluded to by the first seal.

If this vision were read independently, it would not remind one of the plagues against the Egyptians. Since the exodus story has already been evoked in this cycle, the reader naturally looks for some correspondence between the sixth trumpet and one of the earlier plagues. The closest parallel is the tenth plague, in which all of the first-born in Egypt were slain, including human beings (Exodus 11-12). Here, a third of humanity is slain.

This vision has a strangely incongruous character, like a dream. The previous vision had much the same quality. We have already noted one aspect of the vision following the sixth trumpet—it seems to describe the assembling of a great army for battle. Alongside that imagery is the remark that it is the *four angels* who were destined to kill a third of humanity (vs. 15). In addition, the horses of the cavalry are described as supernatural agents of destruction, like the locusts of the fifth trumpet. Their heads are *like lion's heads, and fire and smoke and sulphur issued from their mouths.* The fire, smoke and sulphur are said to cause the deaths of a third of humanity. As the locusts sting like scorpions, so the horses wound *like serpents.*

It is unlikely that this vision was intended to be an accurate prediction of some future event or events. It is a dim, fragmentary and mysterious picture of a crisis. The crisis is portrayed in a way which expresses great confidence in divine providence and justice.

Just as the Egyptians stubbornly resisted the divine will, so does John expect humanity to continue in its idolatrous obstinacy. Verses 20-21 express the prophet's conviction that the people of his day were so alienated from the creator that no crisis could move them to repentance. Events in which the faithful would see divine providence and justice are simply acts of blind fate to others.

JOHN IS COMMISSIONED A SECOND TIME.
10.

10 Then I saw another mighty angel coming down from heaven, wrapped in a cloud, with a rainbow over his head, and his face was like the sun, and his legs like pillars of fire. [2]He had a little scroll open in his hand. And he set his right foot on the sea, and his left foot on the land, [3]and called out with a loud voice, like a lion roaring; when he called out, the seven thunders sounded. [4]And when the seven thunders had sounded, I was about to write, but I heard a voice from heaven saying, "Seal up what the seven thunders have said, and do not write it down." [5]And the angel whom I saw standing on sea and land lifted up his right hand to heaven [6]and swore by him who lives for ever and ever, who created heaven and what is in it, the earth and what is in it, and the sea and what is in it, that there should be no more delay, [7]but that in the days of the trumpet call to be sounded by the seventh angel, the mystery of God, as he announced to his servants the prophets, should be fulfilled.

[8]Then the voice which I had heard from heaven spoke to me again, saying, "Go, take the scroll which is open in the hand of the angel who is standing on the sea and on the land." [9]So I went to the angel and told him to give me the little scroll; and he said to me, "Take it and eat; it will be bitter to your stomach, but sweet as honey in your mouth." [10]And I took the little scroll from the hand of the angel and ate it; it was sweet as honey in my mouth, but when I had eaten it my stomach was made bitter. [11]And I was told, "You must again prophesy about many peoples and nations and tongues and kings."

The vision of the sixth trumpet is followed by a vision of a *mighty angel* (10:1-11), which is not linked to one of the seven trumpets. Like the two visions of the salvation of the faithful in chapter 7, this vision and 11:1-13 form a kind of interlude in the cycle of the trumpets.

The purpose of this interlude does not seem to be primarily a matter of emphasis, as was the case in chapter 7. These two visions have a particular role to play in the literary structure of the Apocalypse as a whole. Chapter 10 introduces the second part of the book, chapters 12-22.

The vision in 11:1-13 foreshadows the content of the second half of the Apocalypse. In effect, these two visions belong to the second part of the book. They are placed within the trumpet cycle in order to link the two halves of the Apocalypse to each other. This linking or interlocking is a literary device. It balances the device of repetition, of beginning again with a new series of seven. The beginning of a new series of seven is a signal that a new story is about to be told. The links between the cycles show that all the shorter stories form a greater whole. They are really different versions of the same story of the end-time.

We noted earlier that John is commissioned by Christ in the initial vision of the Apocalypse (1:9 - 3:22). In 1:11 Christ commands him to write what he sees in a book and send it to the seven churches. The commission is continued in 1:19, when John is told to write what he sees, "what is and what is to take place hereafter." At the beginning of the vision of the heavenly council, a voice tells John that he will be shown "what must take place after this" (4:1). This repetition of the commission in 1:19 shows that John was commanded to share not only the seven messages but the visions connected with the seven seals as well.

In chapter 10 John is commissioned a second time, in this case by an angel. The angel *had a little scroll open in his hand.* John is commanded to *Go, take the scroll which is open in the hand of the angel . . . .* John *took the scroll from the hand of the angel and ate it.* The image of the angel giving the scroll to the prophet implies that the angel gives him the message he is to announce. In other words, the prophetic message has a heavenly origin. The eating of the scroll is a symbolic action. It shows in a vivid and concrete way that the prophet does not announce his own message, but one which comes from outside himself.

After John has eaten the scroll, he is commanded to prophesy *again*. This wording implies that John has fulfilled his first commission and is being issued a new one.

The new commission makes chapter 10 parallel to chapter 1. Chapter 10 is also parallel to chapter 5. In chapter 10 John sees *another mighty angel*. The first "mighty angel" appeared in chapter 5 and asked "Who is worthy to open the scroll and break its seals?" Both visions involve a heavenly book. The *sealed* scroll of chapter 5 is contrasted with the *open* scroll of chapter 10. But they are handled in similar ways. The sealed scroll is in the hand of the enthroned one (5:1). The open scroll is in the hand of the mighty angel (10:2,8). The lamb "went and took the scroll from the right hand of him who was seated on the throne. And when he had taken the scroll . . . ." (5:7-8). Similarly, John *went to the angel . . .* and *took the little scroll from the hand of the angel . . . and when [he] had eaten it . . .* (10:9-10). These parallels imply that the visions of the seals and trumpets reveal the content of the sealed scroll, whereas the visions beginning with 12:1 disclose the message of the open scroll. The contrasting images of "sealed" and "open" hint that the second half of the Apocalypse will give a more detailed version of the story of the end-time.

Some commentators have argued that 11:1-13 already reveals the content of the little scroll mentioned in chapter 10. This theory is less likely than the one argued above. The vision in 11:1-13 has its own symbolic action—the measuring of the temple. The rest of the vision interpets that action, not the symbolic action of chapter 10. Further, the commission in 10:11 calls for a prophecy about *many kings*. This reference fits chapters 13 and 17 better than 11:1-13.

A major function of chapter 10 is to introduce the second part of the Apocalypse and to link it to the first part. Another function is to build suspense for the sounding of the seventh trumpet and to interpret its effects. The description of the mighty angel is inspired in part by the vision of Dan 12:5-13. Three angels appear in Daniel's vision—one on each bank of the river and another above the waters. John sees a single angel covering an analogous, though larger and cosmically symbolic, space—*his right foot on the sea, and his left foot on the land . . . .* The corresponding vision in Daniel is the last one in the book. The seer asks, "O my Lord, what shall be the issue of these things?" The angel replies that he will be given no further revelation, "Go your way, Daniel, for the words are shut up and sealed until the time of the end (Dan 12:9). The angel's refusal to give more details implies that the revelation given is only partial. The mysteries of the hidden aspects of reality and of the future are too great to be revealed fully to humanity.

The vision of Revelation 10 has a similar message. Soon after the appearance of the angel *the seven thunders sounded.* A voice tells John not to write down what the seven thunders said. Here, near the end of one of the Apocalypse's stories of the end, a heavenly voice reveals that the story is only partial. It is not given to humanity to receive complete revelation of the mysteries of what is and what is to come.

In the last vision of Daniel, the seer asks another question, this one about the timing of the end (12:6). The angel's answer, introduced by an oath, is given in veiled but apparently specific terms—the end will come in about three and a half years (literally "times," 12:7; see also 12:11). Daniel's response is "I heard, but I did not understand" (12:8). It is likely that John was reinterpreting that passage and applying it to his own time. He probably thought that Dan 12:5-13 was a prophecy of the great turning point which he himself expected in the near future. It is likely that the author and first readers of Daniel understood the three and a half years literally. It is less likely that John and his first readers did. The three and a half years, expressed in various forms, in the Apocalypse is probably a symbolic figure for a short time of woe (11:2,3; 12:6,14; 13:5).

After the reference to the seven thunders, the mighty angel swears an oath very similar to the one sworn by the angel in Dan 12:7. As in Daniel, the oath is followed by a revelation of the timing of the end. Here, the period of time mentioned in Daniel is not used. No particular dates or periods of time are mentioned, although the sense of urgency is apparent: *there should be no more delay, but that in the days of the trumpet call to be sounded by the seventh angel, the mystery of God, as he announced to his servants the prophets, should be fulfilled.* On one level, the *mystery* refers to God's providential control of the future. On another level, it probably refers to older, apparently unfulfilled prophecies like Daniel 12. The saying of the angel does not encourage new calculations of the exact time at which the present order will end. The time of the seventh trumpet is itself symbolic and inexact. The angel's saying does encourage trust in providence and in the validity of Scripture. But it also implies the need to reassess older revelation in terms of the present situation.

THE DESTINY OF GOD'S WITNESSES.
11:1-13.

11 Then I was given a measuring rod like a staff, and I was told: "Rise and measure the temple of God and the altar and those who worship there, 2but do not measure the court outside the temple; leave that out, for it is given over to the nations, and they will trample over the holy city for forty-two months. 3And I will grant my two witnesses power to prophesy for one thousand two hundred and sixty days, clothed in sackcloth."

4These are the two olive trees and the two lampstands which stand before the Lord of the earth. 5And if any one would harm them, fire pours from their mouth and consumes their foes: if any one would harm them, thus he is doomed to be killed. 6They have power to shut the sky, that no rain may fall during the days of their prophesying, and they have power over the waters to turn them into blood, and to smite the earth with every plague, as often as they desire. 7And when they have finished their testimony, the beast that ascends from the bottomless pit will make war upon them and conquer them and kill them, 8and their dead bodies will lie in the street of the great city which is allegorically called Sodom and Egypt, where their Lord was crucified. 9For three days and a half men from the peoples and tribes and tongues and nations gaze at their dead bodies and refuse to let them be placed in a tomb, [10]and those who dwell on the earth will rejoice over them and make merry and exchange presents, because these two prophets had been a torment to those who dwell on the earth. [11]But after the three and a half days a breath of life from God entered them, and they stood up on their feet, and great fear fell on those who saw them. [12]Then they heard a loud voice from heaven saying to them, "Come up hither!" And in the sight of their foes they went up to heaven in a cloud. [13]And at that hour there was a great earthquake, and a tenth of the city fell; seven thousand people were killed in the earthquake, and the rest were terrified and gave glory to the God of heaven.

As suggested above, the vision of 11:1-13 foreshadows the content of the second part of the Apocalypse, chapters 12-22. The characters and events are much more similar to the second half of the book than to anything we have met so far. Especially the sudden and cryptic reference to *the beast* (vs. 7) points ahead to the way the story of the end will be told in chapters 12-22. The reason for placing 11:1-13 here is to link the first part of the Apocalypse with the second. The link shows that they are not two totally independent stories, but different versions of the same story.

John is given a *measuring rod* and told to *measure the temple of God and the altar and those who worship there.* This new symbolic action sets 11:1-13 off as a distinct unit from chapter 10. The command to measure is balanced by a command not to measure the *court outside the temple.* No purpose is given for the act of measuring. A reason is given for refraining from measuring the court—*it is given over to the nations, and they will trample over the holy city for forty-two months.* The implied reason for measuring the temple, the altar and the worshippers then must be to express the promise that they will not be given over to the nations.

The meaning of this symbolic action has been much debated. One major opinion is that the *temple* is the earthly temple in Jerusalem and the worshippers are people who took control of the temple during the first revolt against Rome (66-70 A.D.). These people were members of the Zealot movement and may have included some Jewish-Christians. Some who hold this interpretation think that 11:1-2 is an independent oracle composed in Zealot circles before the destruction of the temple and the city of Jerusalem in 70 A.D. They argue that the passage must be prior to 70, since it reflects no idea of the destruction of Jerusalem, only of its capture. Others who interpret the passage in the same way consider it evidence that the whole book was composed before 70 A.D.

It is unlikely that the Apocalypse as a whole was written before the destruction of Jerusalem and its temple. The promise that the conquerors would be pillars in the temple of God (3:12) and the lack of a temple in the vision of salvation at the end of the book (21:22) imply that the temple had been destroyed and ways found to understand and accept its absence. It is possible that 11:1-2 had an independent existence prior to its use in the Apocalypse. Even if it had, the reader of the Apocalypse must be able to understand it in its present context.

The nations will trample the holy city for *forty-two months*. This time period is equivalent to the three and a half times or years mentioned in Dan 12:7. In discussing chapter 10, we noted that this period in the Apocalypse stands for the time of tribulation immediately preceding the end. It is likely that John considered himself to be living already in that time of woe. In any case, it is a *period* of time not a particular *point* of time. It is likely then, that here it refers generally to the Roman persecution of Christians and not specifically to the repression of the first Jewish revolt.

If this interpretation is correct, then the saying should be read metaphorically, not literally. One should not debate whether the earthly, heavenly or future temple is meant. The saying implies that, on one level, the people who worship God are being oppressed by an illegitimate imperial power. But this oppression is not able to destroy the relationship these people have with their Lord. The presence of God, symbolized by the temple and the altar, is still felt by them in the midst of their troubles.

Suddenly, following the commands to measure and to refrain from measuring, the *two witnesses* are introduced. They are to *prophesy for one thousand two hundred and sixty days*. Like the forty-two months in 11:2, this time period is equivalent to the three and a half years of Daniel. Since the witnesses are killed for their testimony, it is likely that their ministry is set in the same final period of woe referred to in 11:2.

The witnesses are identified as *the two olive trees and the two lampstands which stand before the Lord of the earth*. This identification calls to mind one of the visions of Zechariah. The prophet sees "two branches of the olive trees" and "two golden pipes from which the oil is poured out" (Zech 4:12). An angel tells him that these represent "the two anointed who stand by the Lord of the whole earth" (Zech 4:14). Once again, John is using an old story, traditional images, to interpret his own situation. In the context of Zechariah, the two anointed are the new Davidic ruler and the new high priest.

The context in the Apocalypse, however, does not imply the coming of a Davidic and a priestly messiah. The passage from Zechariah is to be fulfilled in a way the prophet did not foresee. The activity of each of the witnesses recalls the mighty deeds of Moses and Elijah, as well as the ministry and destiny of Jesus. If *any one would harm them*, they have power to destroy *their foes by fire*. This element recalls one of the stories about Elijah (2 Kings 1:9-12, Sir 48:3). Their *power to shut the sky, that no rain may fall during the days of their prophesying* recalls an even more famous story about Elijah (1 Kings 17-18, Sir 48:3, Lk 4:25, James 5:17). The *power over the waters to turn them into blood, and to smite the earth with every plague* recalls the role of Moses as God's agent in smiting the Egyptians, especially his turning the Nile and all the waters in Egypt into blood (Ex 7:14-19).

The two witnesses will be killed in Jerusalem, where *their Lord was crucified*. Their bodies will lie unburied for *three days and a half*; then God will bring them back to life (vs. 11). Finally, they will go up to heaven in a cloud (vs. 12). The basic pattern of the witnesses' destiny very clearly repeats that of Jesus' ministry: a prophetic ministry including mighty deeds, violent death in. Jerusalem, resurrection after three days and ascension. The ascension of the two witnesses also reminds the reader of Elijah's ascension in a chariot (2 Kings 2:11). Moses was also thought to have ascended into heaven. Such a tradition is probably referred to in Jude 9.

Many theories have been proposed on the identity of the two witnesses and the time of their appearance. One theory is that they are historical figures, Peter and Paul. Another theory holds that the vision is an unfulfilled prophecy of the return of Moses and Elijah or of two super-human forerunners of the second coming of Christ. It is difficult to determine how John understood this vision. One can ask, in any case, how the story expressed in this vision probably functioned for him and his first readers. We might call this vision the story of the two witnesses. Their story, like the story about Jesus, provides a point of orientation for the readers. Like the two characters in the story, the readers aspire to being God's witnesses, to giving *testimony* about God's cause in the world. They too are confident of God's protection, even though they may be called upon to endure hardships, suffering, even violent death. God's protection is expected in their every-day lives and beyond and in spite of death. This protection is described in spectacular ways in the story. This spectacular divine intervention expresses in a symbolic way the deep trust that the cause of the witnesses is just and real and worth dying for.

The *beast* who kills the witnesses *ascends from the bottomless pit*. The origin of the beast in the pit recalls the vision of the fifth trumpet, when the fallen angel opened the bottomless pit and released the locusts. We noted that the story of the fifth trumpet is an adaptation of the story of the fallen angels. The releasing of the locusts symbolizes the revival of evil forces which had been temporarily confined by the forces of creation and order. Here, the beast has the same symbolic function as the locusts. The ascension of the beast from the pit implies that the forces which oppose the testimony of God's witnesses are part of the constant struggle of death with life, of destruction with creation, of evil with good. We will discover more about the beast in chapter 13.

It is likely that Jerusalem, *the great city*, represents the Jewish people who have not recognized Jesus as God's agent. The reference to Jerusalem as *Sodom and Egypt* is a prophetic admonition in the spirit of Is 1:10. It is born out of the controversy reflected in the messages to Smyrna (2:9) and Philadelphia (3:9), where the Jews are called a synagogue of Satan. The end of the story in 11:13 implies that John is hopeful of the ultimate conversion of the Jews. Unlike the general population who suffer from the plagues of the sixth trumpet, the dwellers in Jerusalem repent when they perceive God's powerful intervention.

THE MANIFESTATION OF THE KINGDOM OF GOD. 11:14-19.

[14]The second woe has passed; behold, the third woe is soon to come.

[15]Then the seventh angel blew his trumpet, and there were loud voices in heaven, saying, "The kingdom of the world has become the kingdom of our Lord and of his Christ, and he shall reign for ever and ever." [16]And the twenty-four elders who sit on their thrones before God fell on their faces and worshiped God, [17]saying,

"We give thanks to thee, Lord God Almighty, who art and who wast,

☐ that thou hast taken thy great power and begun to reign.

[18]The nations raged, but thy wrath came,
and the time for the dead to be judged,
for rewarding thy servants, the prophets and saints,

and those who fear thy name, both small and great,
and for destroying the destroyers of the earth."
[19]Then God's temple in heaven was opened, and the
ark of his covenant was seen within his temple; and there
were flashes of lightning, loud noises, peals of thunder,
and earthquake, and heavy hail.

After the fourth trumpet, John saw an eagle in heaven,
which proclaimed the last three trumpets as woes upon those
who dwell on the earth (8:13). After the interlude of 10:1-
11:13, we are reminded that the *second woe has passed*,
the sixth trumpet, and that *the third woe is soon to come*.
The seventh trumpet is a woe for *the nations* who will feel
God's *wrath* and for *the destroyers of the earth* who will
be destroyed themselves.

Like the visions of the seals, the cycle of the trumpets
also tells the entire story of the end. Both versions of the
story contain the pattern of persecution, judgment and
triumph. The transitional vision (8:3-5) which links the
two cycles alludes to persecution with its references to the
"altar" and the "prayers of the saints." These references
recall the souls under the altar who were killed for their
testimony (6:9-11). Both of the last two elements of the
pattern are expressed in the seventh trumpet. Judgment
against the nations, destruction of the destroyers of the
earth and the general judgment of the dead are all proclaimed in the hymn of the elders (vs.18). Salvation is
expressed in the proclamation that the *kingdom of the world
has become the kingdom of our Lord and of his Christ, and
he shall reign for ever and ever.* This manifestation of the
kingdom of God is salvation from a cosmic point of view.
Salvation from an individual point of view is expressed in
the announcement of the *rewarding* of God's *servants, the
prophets and saints, and those who fear thy name, both
small and great . . . .*
Like the vision of the triumph of the faithful near the
end of the seals, the seventh trumpet introduces a heavenly

scene. In both cases salvation is expressed by means of a heavenly liturgy. The multitude praised God along with the angels (7:9-12) for bringing salvation and triumph. Here *loud voices* and the *twenty-four elders* proclaim the joyful news.

Compared with the second part of the Apocalypse, chapters 1-11 give a fragmentary and veiled view of the judgment and salvation being revealed. Thus it is fitting that the first part end with the bare announcement of the kingdom of God. Few images are used to flesh out that proclamation. Here we are given only the outline of what is to be painted with rich colors in the second part. Part one concludes with a cryptic but powerful epiphany of the *ark* of God's covenant in the heavenly *temple*—a majestic though indirect manifestation of the presence of God.

Part II
THE OPEN SCROLL.
12-22.

THE SECOND PART of the Apocalypse is introduced by the vision of chapter 10 in which a mighty angel gives John his second commission. The revelation in this second half of the book is symbolized by the little scroll which the angel gives him to eat. John is told, "You must again prophesy about many peoples and nations and tongues and kings."

The vision of 11:1-13 gives a preview of the content of the second part of the Apocalypse. The story of the two witnesses illustrates the destiny of those who bear testimony to God and the lamb. Their destiny, like Jesus', involves both suffering and glory. The beast who ascends from the bottomless pit appears for the first time in the story of the two witnesses. He will be a major character in the second half of the Apocalypse.

As was suggested earlier, the Apocalypse as a whole is a narrative made up of many short narratives. Each vision is a story and these miniature stories are combined into cycles, each of which tells the same basic account of the end of the world. The three cycles of part two tell this story, each from a different perspective. Like the cycles of part one, those of part two are linked to one another. These links are literary devices which provide the opportunity to tell another version of the story. They also prevent the conclusion that any of the stories is independent of the others.

Chapters 12-22 contain three cycles of visions: (1) the first unnumbered cycle (12:1 - 15:4), (2) the seven bowls plus the Bablyon appendix (15:5 - 19:10), and (3) the second unnumbered cycle plus the Jerusalem appendix (19:11 - 22:5). The first two are linked in a way similar to the interlocking of the seals and the trumpets in part one. The placement and function of the vision of the triumphant faithful in 15:2-4 are similar to those of the vision of the angel with the censer in 8:3-5. The vision of the triumph of the faithful in heaven (15:2-4) is the climactic seventh vision of the first unnumbered cycle (12:1 - 15:4). It is also a transitional vision, because of its insertion into the introduction of the seven bowls (15:1,5-8).

The cycle of the seven bowls is linked to the last cycle by the parallelism between the Babylon appendix and the Jerusalem appendix (17:1 - 19:10 and 21:9 - 22:5). Formally, they are very similar. Each is introduced by a scene in which one of the angels who had the seven bowls comes to John and says, "Come, I will show you . . . ." In each case he shows him a symbolic woman, after John is carried away to his vantage point by the Spirit.

The content of the two appendices creates a stark contrast. The two women have the names of two cities. The new Babylon is portrayed as a harlot, the new Jerusalem as a pure bride. Each city symbolizes a people and a way of life. Babylon represents those who ally themselves with the city of Rome and her imperial values. Jerusalem represents the followers of Jesus and the christian life.

The links between the cycles of chapters 12-22 also show that these chapters form a literary unity, just as chapters 1-11 do. These two major parts of the book are telling the same basic story, as has been noted. The difference between the two is that part one introduces and hints at what part two reveals more fully. The relationship between the two parts can be illustrated by showing how a major theme of the book is developed.

One major theme in the Apocalypse is the theme of Jesus as the messiah. This theme is introduced already in the greeting near the beginning of the book—he is "the ruler of kings on earth" (1:5). The messianic rule of Jesus is described as a present reality also in the promise to the conquerors in the message to Thyatira (2:26-27). In view of the experiences of hardship facing the seven churches, the claim that Jesus already rules the kings of the earth is puzzling. The resolution of the puzzle begins in chapter 5. The messianic titles "the lion of the tribe of Judah" and "the root of David" are reinterpreted in terms of the death of Jesus, which is his conquest. The death of Jesus is the beginning of his defeat of Satan. But the reader does not yet know how this conquest relates to the kings of the earth.

The puzzle of the messianic theme is resolved on a narrative level in part two. Chapter 12 tells the story of the birth of a child whom the readers would identify as Jesus. This child will rule the nations as messiah at some future time (12:5). The exercise of that rule "with a rod of iron" is described in the great battle between the forces of Christ and those of the beast (19:11-21). The climax of the messianic theme is the vision of Christ's reign for a thousand years (20:4-6).

The references to the future rule of Christ in part two seem to contradict the statements of his present rule in part one. The key to this apparent contradiction lies in recognizing that the future rule of Christ is expressed in *stories*. They should not be read as literal descriptions of events which will occur in the future. Stories are told to interpret and shape the present. The narratives about Jesus' defeat of Satan and the beast imply that the way of life Jesus stood for is more real, true and just than the way of life represented by the beast. For these reasons, the Christian way of life is even more powerful than the power of the beast, although some would not recognize its power.

The stories of part two then show how and why the messianic claims of part one can be made—that Jesus is the ruler of the kings of the earth. Another theme which illustrates the relationship between the two parts is the theme of the rebellion of Satan. This theme is central in the first cycle of part two.

A. THE CHURCH IN A COSMIC CONFLICT. 12:1 - 15:4.

THE STORY of the rebellion of Satan against God is one of the stories told to explain the disorder and evil of the present. This story is hinted at a number of times in part one of the Apocalypse. When Satan rebels, he is thrown out of heaven. One of the results of his downfall is that he tries to persuade human beings to join him in rebelling against heaven. When the apocalyptic mentality is at work, this element of the story is adapted to a dualistic way of thinking. All humanity is divided into those who are loyal to God and those who join Satan's revolt. There is no middle ground. Such apocalyptic thinking is reflected in the references to synagogues of Satan (2:9,3:9). The implication is that the Jews of Smyrna and Philadelphia have joined Satan in rebelling against God. The messages do not make very clear just how they have done so.

The message to Pergamum says that Satan dwells there and has his throne there. The presence of a throne of Satan on earth implies a rebellious kingdom of Satan in opposition to the kingdom of God. Satan's throne (2:13) is contrasted with God's throne (4:2). Satan's rebellious kingdom is associated with the death of Antipas in Pergamum. The precise connection between the two is not expressed.

We noted earlier that chapter 5 portrays a crisis in the heavenly council over the lack of someone worthy and able to open the scroll with seven seals. This crisis is intelligible when the reader understands that the rebellion of Satan is presupposed. This rebellion is a major narrative theme in the first cycle of unnumbered visions (12:1-15:4).

THE DRAGON'S ATTACK.
12.

12 And a great portent appeared in heaven, a woman clothed with the sun, with the moon under her feet, and on her head a crown of twelve stars; ²she was with child and she cried out in her pangs of birth, in anguish for delivery. ³And another portent appeared in heaven; behold, a great red dragon, with seven heads and ten horns, and seven diadems upon his heads. ⁴His tail swept down a third of the stars of heaven, and cast them to the earth. And the dragon stood before the woman who was about to bear a child, that he might devour her child when she brought it forth; ⁵she brought forth a male child, one who is to rule all the nations with a rod of iron, but her child was caught up to God and to his throne, ⁶and the woman fled into the wilderness, where she has a place prepared by God, in which to be nourished for one thousand two hundred and sixty days.

⁷Now war arose in heaven, Michael and his angels fighting against the dragon; and the dragon and his angels fought, ⁸but they were defeated and there was no longer any place for them in heaven. ⁹And the great dragon was thrown down, that ancient serpent, who is called the Devil and Satan, the deceiver of the whole world—he was thrown down to the earth, and his angels were thrown down with him. ¹⁰And I heard a loud voice in heaven, saying, "Now the salvation and the power and the kingdom of our God and the authority of his Christ have come, for the accuser of our brethren has been thrown down, who accuses them day and night before our God. ¹¹And they have conquered him by the blood of the Lamb and by the word of their testimony, for they loved not their lives even unto death. ¹²Rejoice then, O heaven and you that dwell therein! But woe to you, O earth and

sea, for the devil has come down to you in great wrath, because he knows that his time is short!"

¹³And when the dragon saw that he had been thrown down to the earth, he pursued the woman who had borne the male child. ¹⁴But the woman was given the two wings of the great eagle that she might fly from the serpent into the wilderness, to the place where she is to be nourished for a time, and times, and half a time. ¹⁵The serpent poured water like a river out of his mouth after the woman, to sweep her away with the flood. ¹⁶But the earth came to the help of the woman, and the earth opened its mouth and swallowed the river which the dragon had poured from his mouth. ¹⁷Then the dragon was angry with the woman, and went off to make war on the rest of her offspring, on those who keep the commandments of God and bear testimony to Jesus. And he stood on the sand of the sea.

The opening vision of this cycle is a story about one stage of Satan's rebellion. This story is allegorical in the sense of having more than one level of meaning. One of the major characters in the story is the *dragon.* We are told that this dragon is the *ancient serpent, who is called the Devil and Satan, the deceiver of the whole world.* This vision is an example of the way John uses an old story to fashion a new one.

The ancient story of cosmic combat is the "old story" adapted in this vision. The story usually begins with the revolt of a divine or cosmic beast against the divine hero who is the universal king. The purpose of the revolt is to seize kingship. The rule of the hero is characterized by justice, order and fertility. The beast stands for the opposing qualities—lawlessness, chaos and sterility. The battle between the two is a cosmic conflict in which order in nature and among people is at stake.

In some forms of the story, the beast attempts to prevent a young hero from coming to power. In these cases, the attack is directed against the hero's mother while she is pregnant with him or against the hero as a defenseless infant. The story of chapter 12 of the Apocalypse is of this type.

The *great red dragon*, on one level of meaning, is the rebellious beast who wants to become universal king. His association with chaos is shown by his threat to the order of the cosmos: *His tail swept down a third of the stars of heaven, and cast them to the earth.* The woman is portrayed as a high goddess, Queen of Heaven; she is *clothed with the sun, with the moon under her feet, and on her head a crown of twelve stars.* She is in the throes of labor and the child about to be born is destined to be the universal king—*one who is to rule all the nations with a rod of iron.* The dragon's revolt consists in an attempt to prevent the child from fulfilling his kingly destiny; he *stood before the woman ... that he might devour her child when she brought it forth.*

In some stories of combat, it is not the hero himself who actually fights the beast. Often some ally accomplishes that task for him. The child in this vision has such an ally, *Michael,* one of the seven archangels. Michael's victory over the dragon, however, is partial. The dragon is defeated in heaven but he exercises his reign on earth. He renews his revolt by pursuing *the woman who had borne the male child.*

It is at this point that the story of chapter 12 becomes very similar to one particular story of cosmic combat. It is the story of the dragon Python's attempt to prevent the coming to power of Apollo, the son of Zeus by Leto. Python pursues Leto, while she is pregnant with Apollo, in order to kill her. By order of Zeus, the north wind rescues Leto by carrying her off to an island. Then Poseidon, god of the sea, hides her by covering the island with waves. Python cannot find her and so gives up his search.

Here, the woman is apparently helped by order of God (vs.6). As Leto is carried off by the north wind, the woman is *given the two wings of the great eagle that she might fly from the serpent into the wilderness.* As Poseidon came to Leto's aid, the woman is helped by *the earth.* The earth is personified in the story and opens *its mouth* to swallow the flood of water which the dragon had spewed at her. The dragon, though *angry with the woman*, gives up his attack on her. He continues his revolt, however, by attacking *the rest of her offspring.*

It is not surprising that John expresses his vision in terms of the story of conflict between Python and Apollo. In the early Roman empire, Apollo was associated with the mythical "golden age." Apollo's kingship at the beginning of time was the original golden age of wisdom, peace and prosperity. The first emperor, Augustus, and his supporters made use of this tradition and claimed that Augustus' rule was the new golden age and that he was the new Apollo. Several emperors who followed him including Nero, made the same claim about their rules. Nero apparently alluded to a story like the one about Python and Leto, when he claimed that he was threatened by a serpent as an infant.

John's adoption of this story probably had a polemical purpose. His first readers would think of Jesus when reading about the child who would rule the nations. The implication then is that it is Christ and not the emperor who brings the new golden age. It is the christian life which manifests wisdom, peace and true prosperity, not a life shaped by the values of imperial Rome.

On another level of meaning, the vision of chapter 12 recalls the traditional story of Satan's rebellion against God. This story is, in terms of origin, another form of the ancient story of combat. The purpose of Satan's rebellion is to take over God's role as universal king. He persuades a number of other angels to join him in his revolt. The result is a great battle in heaven between the angels loyal to God, led by Michael, and the rebellious angels, led by Satan. The outcome of the battle is that Satan and his followers are cast out of heaven. This story seems to have been told to explain the origin of evil. Excluded from heaven, Satan continues his revolt by persuading human beings to join him in rebelling against God's rule.

John, along with others of his time, apparently read Genesis 3 as an account of such a continuation of Satan's rebellion. John's reference to *that ancient serpent* (vs.9) calls Genesis 3 to mind. Some texts from about John's time say that the serpent was the tool of Satan. John actually identifies the serpent with Satan, perhaps influenced by the serpentine image of the dragon.

So John has made use of two older stories to tell a new story. The purpose of the new story is to interpret the present situation of his first readers and to encourage them to take a particular stand. Some commentators think that each detail in the story of chapter 12 refers to an historical event in John's immediate past. Others think that the story is intended to express abstract and universal truths. John's intention was probably neither of those, but something in between them.

Whatever his intention was, the most illuminating way to read the story is as a paradigm or model of and for the experience of the first readers. They are expected to identify with the woman. The dragon's attack symbolizes their experiences of hardship, alienation from the dominant cultural values, and, for some, arrest, punishment and even execution. The identification of the dragon with Satan implies that their hardships are not meaningless, random events; rather, they result from a systematic and universal tension between order and chaos, good and evil.

The rescue of the woman evokes trust that these hardships are not in vain. The manner of rescue involves themes from the exodus story, as well as parallels to the Leto story. The *two wings of the great eagle* recalls a traditional metaphor for the deliverance from Egypt—"You have seen what I did to the Egyptians, and how I bore you on eagles' wings and brought you to myself" (Ex 19:4). The refuge taken in the desert calls to mind the wilderness wandering. In John's time, retreat to the desert symbolized readiness for the manifestation of God's rule. This figurative account of rescue does not necessarily imply literal protection from harm. In the context of the Apocalypse as a whole, it expresses a radiant trust in divine providence even in the midst of hardship and suffering.

The interpretation of chapter 12 just offered does not try to identify the woman clothed with the sun as many other interpretations do. She has been identified with Mary, the mother of Jesus, with the Church, with Israel and with Jerusalem. But her importance for the Apocalypse lies not so much in her identity as in her destiny. Like the story of the two witnesses of 11:1-13, her story is told to help the readers understand and respond to their own situation. This approach does not deny the validity of attempts to identify the woman. Each of the interpretations mentioned has its strong points. But such identification should have a secondary role in the attempt to understand the vision. It should be seen as a story which interprets the first readers' experience.

This interpretation of the function of the story is supported by the victory song (vss.10-12) which celebrates Satan's fall from heaven. The image of the heavenly court dominates the song. Satan is identified as *the accuser* of the followers of Jesus, the one who tries to persuade God, as heavenly judge, to find them guilty and deserving of punishment. This trial language probably reflects the situation of John and his first readers, threatened with accusation and conviction in the local Roman courts. According to the song, Satan's fall from heaven is, at least in part, a figurative expression of their "conquest," their acquittal in the heavenly court. Their heavenly "acquittal" is based, ironically, on their conviction in the Roman courts. They have stood by *the word of their testimony* and *they loved not their lives even unto death*. This endurance is made possible by the model of Jesus. Therefore, their conquest is also *by the blood of the lamb*.

The victory song of vss. 10-12 makes clear that the Apocalypse associates the story of Satan's rebellion with the trials the first readers must undergo. The same association was implied by the reference to Antipas' execution near Satan's throne (2:13). Chapter 13 illuminates this association further.

SATAN'S VICEROY:
THE BEAST FROM THE SEA.
13:1-10.

13 And I saw a beast rising out of the sea, with ten horns and seven heads, with ten diadems upon its horns and a blasphemous name upon its heads. ²And the beast that I saw was like a leopard, its feet were like a bear's, and its mouth was like a lion's mouth. And to it the dragon gave his power and his throne and great authority. ³One of its heads seemed to have a mortal wound, but its mortal wound was healed, and the whole earth followed the beast with wonder. ⁴Men worshiped the dragon, for he had given his authority to the beast, and they worshiped the beast, saying, "Who is like the beast, and who can fight against it?"

⁵And the beast was given a mouth uttering haughty and blasphemous words, and it was allowed to exercise authority for forty-two months; ⁶it opened its mouth to utter blasphemies against God, blaspheming his name and his dwelling, that is, those who dwell in heaven. ⁷Also it was allowed to make war on the saints and to conquer them. And authority was given it over every tribe and people and tongue and nation, ⁸and all who dwell on earth will worship it, every one whose name has not been written before the foundation of the world in the book of life of the Lamb that was slain. ⁹If any one has an ear, let him hear:

¹⁰If any one is to be taken captive, to captivity he goes;

if any one slays with the sword, with the sword must he be slain.

Here is a call for the endurance and faith of the saints.

Like the vision of chapter 12, this vision is an allegorical story because it invites the reader to understand it on several levels of meaning simultaneously. On one level, it is a re-interpretation of the prophecy of Daniel 7, a vision of four beasts rising out of the sea, each different from the others (Dan 7:3-7). Here, a single beast is seen, but one which combines features of each of the four beasts of Daniel 7. The beasts of Daniel's vision were probably intended to represent four kingdoms—those of the Babylonians, the Persians, the Medes, and the Greeks. In John's time, the fourth beast of Daniel's vision was often interpreted as the Roman empire.

The description of the activity of the beast in vss. 5-6 alludes to elements in another vision of Daniel (8:10-14). That passage of Daniel is a vision of a he-goat (the Greek kingdom) and its little horn (King Antiochus Epiphanes) whose reign is described as rebellion against God. He attacked the host of heaven, and rebelled against God by "magnifying himself" and interfering with the cult of the temple (Dan 8:10-11). Similarly, the beast in this vision of the Apocalypse blasphemes *those who dwell in heaven*, utters *blasphemies against God* and against *his dwelling*. Both passages include a time limit on the rebel's activity (Dan 8:14—2,300 days; Rev 13:5—42 months).

Apparently, John believes that the prophecies of Daniel were fulfilled in his own time or he found in Daniel a story which provided a model for understanding his own situation. In either case, Daniel is an older story used by John to tell his own.

On another level, this vision is a retelling of the ancient story of the struggle between God and the sea monster; that is, between creation and chaos. Like the dragon in chapter 12, the *beast* represents the forces of destruction, chaos and sterility. His *rising out of the sea* confirms this impression, since the salty sea is traditionally a symbol of chaos.

The motif of rebellion, as we have noted, is a major feature of the story of combat over kingship. The reason for the conflict is most often the attempt of a rebel to seize the power of the hero. The revolt is often expressed in arrogantly prideful statements. Here the beast *was given a mouth uttering haughty and blasphemous words.*

On still another level, the earliest readers would have recognized the beast as a symbol of the Roman empire and also of a particular Roman emperor, probably Nero. The universal authority expressed in vs. 7 would have brought Rome to mind for the readers of John's time—*and authority was given it over every tribe and people and tongue and nation . . . .*

The description of the beast is a parody of Jesus. The same Greek phrase translated here as *seemed to have a mortal wound* is used to describe the lamb in 5:6—"as though it had been slain." The parody is more powerful if the beast is meant to symbolize an individual as well as the Roman empire. The best candidate is Nero (54-68 A.D.). He died a violent death, but there was a legend that he was still alive and would return supported by Parthian armies to regain his rule over Rome. The Jewish Sibylline Oracles adopted this pagan legend and spoke of Nero returning from the realm of the dead as the Antichrist. John seems to be familiar with this tradition and presents Nero as the demonic counterpart of Jesus. It is in view of the legend that he can say, its *mortal wound was healed.*

This new image in chapter 13 gives another level of meaning to "the beast that ascends from the bottomless pit" in 11:7. On one level, that beast is the chaos monster, temporarily defeated by the creator god, reviving and returning from his place of imprisonment to renew his revolt. On another level, he is Nero returning from the land of the dead to renew his godless reign over the great empire of the west.

John has used two older stories, the combat story and Daniel, to tell a new story about the Roman empire. In direct opposition to Roman propaganda, that Rome's rule meant order and peace for the whole world, this vision implies that Roman order is really chaos. It is sterile.

John has gone even further by linking this vision of Rome as beast with the vision of Satan's rebellion in chapter

12—*And to it* (the beast) *the dragon gave his power and his throne and great authority.* The implication is that the Roman empire is an agent of Satan in his rebellion against God. Like the Jews in Smyrna and Philadelphia, Roman officials and their supporters have joined the revolt against heaven. One aspect of the revolt is that the beast makes *war on the saints* and conquers them. This is a veiled allusion to the Roman policy of executing known Christians, a policy begun by Nero. This policy is alluded to again in words reminiscent of Jer 15:2—*If any one is to be taken captive, to captivity he goes* . . . . The Greek manuscripts do not agree on the wording of the rest of the saying. Originally, it may have read, *if any one is to be slain with the sword, with the sword must he be slain.* In vs. 7 it is said that the beast *was allowed* to make war on the saints. This saying indicates that the Apocalypse does not express a radical dualism. Yes, the beast rebels against God, but even that rebellion is part of God's plan. Creation may appear to be out of God's control, but even the persecution of the faithful is within divine providence. The saying, reminiscent of one of the Lord's words to Jeremiah, expresses the same idea. The suffering of the saints is unavoidable and is God's will. So the saying *is a call for the endurance and faith of the saints.*

This vision illuminates the claims in the messages that the Jews of Smyrna and Philadelphia are "synagogues of Satan." If Satan's rebellion is expressed in Rome's persecution of Christians, the Jews' participation in the rebellion probably consists of accusing Christians before the authorities. The statement that Satan gave *his throne* to the beast illuminates a remark in the message to Pergamum. According to the message, Satan's throne is in Pergamum. Since Pergamum was the seat of the Roman government of the province, it is Roman headquarters that are called the "throne of Satan." Antipas' death was associated with Satan's throne in the same message. The reader now knows that Antipas was executed by the Roman governor.

Rome is attacked in this vision not only because of its persecution of Christians. Another charge is made against the beast—men *worshipped the beast, saying, "who is like the beast, and who can fight against it?"* Further, *all who dwell on earth will worship it* .... These indirect accusations are related to the charges of blasphemy in vss. 1,5-6. The emperor cult stands behind these remarks about worship and blasphemy. The emperor cult involved honoring the emperor with religious observances, like sacrifice, burning incense and saying prayers. This religio-political cult was very strong in Asia Minor, the area where the seven churches were. The practice arose in part because of the eastern Mediterranean idea that some human beings are closer to being gods than others. In this type of thinking there is no great gulf between humanity and the gods. It is a very different point of view from the Jewish idea of the radically "other" character of Yahweh.

Given such a mentality, it was natural for the citizens of Asia Minor to express appreciation to the emperor for the benefits of his rule by honoring him as a god. The tremendous accomplishments of Augustus, especially, made him appear superhuman to many. The Apocalypse attacks this mentality bitterly. The implication is that God is the source of all power and that human accomplishments are never to be divorced from the aid given them by divine providence.

The story of the beast from the sea was written to interpret the times for the first readers of the Apocalypse and to encourage and strengthen them in their hardships. As story, the vision has significance beyond the time of its composition, because it has a dynamic which fits other times and places as well. The beast from the sea applies to the perennial desire of human beings to dominate one another. It expresses a lust for power, an hierarchical attitude which is without a sense of mutual human respect. So this story is about what we might call counterfeit power. It reveals the pattern of behavior characteristic of such power. Counterfeit power is self-centered. It behaves as though it were fully autonomous. It demands total allegiance and excessive praise for its accomplishments and is ruthless in crushing those who stand in its way.

FALSE PROPHET:
THE BEAST FROM THE EARTH.
13:11-18.

> [11]Then I saw another beast which rose out of the earth; it had two horns like a lamb and it spoke like a dragon. [12]It exercises all the authority of the first beast in its presence, and makes the earth and its inhabitants worship the first beast, whose mortal wound was healed. [13]It works great signs, even making fire come down from heaven to earth in the sight of men; [14]and by the signs which it is allowed to work in the presence of the beast, it deceives those who dwell on earth, bidding them make an image for the beast which was wounded by the sword and yet lived; [15]and it was allowed to give breath to the image of the beast so that the image of the beast should even speak, and to cause those who would not worship the image of the beast to be slain. [16]Also it causes all, both small and great, both rich and poor, both free and slave, to be marked on the right hand or the forehead, [17]so that no one can buy or sell unless he has the mark, that is, the name of the beast or the number of its name. [18]This calls for wisdom: let him who has understanding reckon the number of the beast, for it is a human number, its number is six hundred and sixty-six.

The beast from the sea of 13:1-10 is contrasted with a beast *which rose out of the earth.* Two beasts or dragons appear as allies in stories of conflict over kingship. The book of Job reflects a story about Leviathan (a beast from the sea) and Behemoth (a beast from the earth), who were defeated by the Creator in primordial time. They represent chaos and disorder and must be held in check constantly to prevent their disruption of the created order. The ongoing battle between God and these beasts is a figurative expression of the constant tension between creation and chaos (see Job 40-41). The story of Leviathan and Behemoth appears in Jewish apocalyptic writings and is probably intended as one level of meaning in chapter 13 of the Apocalypse.

Like the beast from the sea, the beast from the earth is an Antichrist figure. It *had two horns like a lamb*; that is, it claimed allegiance as the true lamb does. But *it spoke like a dragon*—its message and values are not like those of Jesus, but are of Satan.

This second beast *exercises all the authority of the first beast*. This remark implies that the second beast represents the Roman governor or the local political authorities in Asia Minor. It is they who hold the delegated power of the emperor. The second beast also *makes the earth and its inhabitants worship the first beast*. The Roman governors and local political leaders were usually eager to see the emperor cult thrive in the area of their jurisdiction. Such honor to the emperor would enhance their stature in his eyes and help them consolidate their power. So on one level of meaning, the second beast represents the agents of the emperor in ruling Asia Minor.

On another level of meaning, the second beast represents the priests who performed the rituals of the emperor cult. It is they who would be in a position to work *great signs*, to deceive *those who dwell on earth, bidding them make an image for the beast* . . . . Elsewhere in the Apocalypse, the second beast is called "the false prophet" (16:13, 19:20, 20:10). This title fits priests better than political leaders. In describing the cultic activity of the second beast, John makes use of early Christian tradition about false prophets expected to appear during the end-time. According to Mark 13:22, "False Christs and false prophets will arise and show signs and wonders, to lead astray, if possible, the elect."

It is difficult to determine whether John considered the signs mentioned in this vision present or future events. It is striking that he seems to assume that the false prophet actually has or will have miraculous power. He is able to make *fire come down from heaven* and *to give breath to the image of the beast so that the image of the beast should even speak.* These powers are real from John's point of view; the beast *is allowed to work* these signs. So for John, miraculous power in itself is not a sign of divinity or divine favor. Satan and his allies have such power as well as the two witnesses of 11:1-13. It is necessary to discover the origin and purpose of extraordinary power, to evaluate its effects.

The second *beast causes all . . . to be marked on the right hand or the forehead, so that no one can buy or sell unless he has the mark, that is, the name of the beast or the number of its name.* The mark of the beast on the forehead or hand is an image which corresponds to the seal of the living God placed on the foreheads of the faithful. Both images are metaphorical; they do not refer to actual physical marks. The mark of the beast, like the seal of God, symbolizes the allegiance given by the one marked or sealed. Each kind of allegiance brings the appropriate result. The sealed are under God's protection (9:4); those with the mark of the beast are destined for plagues (16:2) and for eternal punishment (14:9-11).

The mark of the beast then is symbolic of allegiance to Rome. Vs. 17 implies that those without the mark were prevented from buying and selling. Now Roman coins generally bore the image and name of the current emperor. Refusal to use such coins at least would inhibit severely one's ability to buy and sell in Asia Minor. Such a refusal by John and his first readers would not be surprising, since the emperor was often pictured as a god on coins. The Zealots, who rebelled against Rome in 66-70 A.D., refused to carry, look at or manufacture coins bearing any sort of image. Their practice was based on a strict interpretation of the first commandment (see Ex 20:4) and on the belief that the images and inscriptions of Roman coins were idolatrous. This vision implies a similar judgment.

In John's time, the letters of the alphabet were used as numbers as well as letters; the letter "a" was "one," "b" was "two," and so forth. It was a common practice, especially in writings intended to be somewhat esoteric, to refer to a person with a number. The number would be the sum of the letters of that person's name. Many different combinations of letters would have the same total. Therefore, the readers had to have independent information about the person being discussed in order to know with certainty who it was. This practice is reflected in the announcement of *the number of the* (first) *beast, . . . its number is six hundred and sixty-six*. On one level of meaning, this is very likely a cryptic reference to Nero. The letters of "Caesar Nero" in Hebrew add up to 666. Several early commentators interpret the number in this way. Also, the letters of the same name in Latin add up to 616; a number of manuscripts of the Apocalypse have 616 instead of 666. Foreign languages were often used to make the reference even more esoteric. This interpretation fits the rest of the chapter with its allusions to the legend that Nero would return. It also fits the most likely interpretation of chapter 17 as we shall see.

On another level of meaning, the number 666 has symbolic connotations. "Seven" symbolizes plentitude and completeness. "Six" has connotations of incompleteness, imperfection, and even of evil.

In this vision of the beast from the earth, the "old story" of cosmic combat has been used once again to interpret the present situation. In this case, the local political authorities and the local imperial priesthood are described as the forces of chaos threatening the stability of God's creation.

The tradition of the "false prophet" who deceives by mighty signs and wonders is also used to characterize the seductive power of the emperor cult. The vision implies that, even for some Christians, the emperor cult was attractive because of its religious power. On another level, it was seductive because of the close links between economic, political and religious aspects of life at the time. Anyone who refused to honor the emperor in a religious way would have severe economic and political problems. The Jews were exempted and this exemption was one reason for the bitter arguments over who were the true Jews.

Like the vision of the beast from the sea, the story of the beast from the earth was written to interpret the times for the earliest readers of the Apocalypse. Because of its figurative character, this vision applies to other circumstances as well. The story of the beast from the earth applies to any situation in which false power demands total allegiance. When it is given, such total allegiance might be called counterfeit cult. This story applies also to churches which simply reflect the current cultural values in an uncritical way. Such an unconscious allegiance is also counterfeit cult.

THE FAITHFUL WHO FOLLOW THE LAMB. 14:1-5.

> **14** Then I looked, and lo, on Mount Zion stood the Lamb, and with him a hundred and forty-four thousand who had his name and his Father's name written on their foreheads. [2]And I heard a voice from heaven like the sound of many waters and like the sound of loud thunder; the voice I heard was like the sound of harpers playing on their harps, [3]and they sing a new song before the throne and before the four living creatures and before the elders. No one could learn that song except the hundred and forty-four thousand who had been redeemed from the earth. [4]It is these who have not defiled themselves with women, for they are chaste; it is these who follow the Lamb wherever he goes; these have been redeemed from mankind as first fruits for God and the Lamb, [5]and in their mouth no lie was found, for they are spotless.

This vision is very difficult to place in space and time; such considerations are probably secondary in understanding the vision's impact. The portrayal of the lamb on

Mount Zion seems at first to locate the vision in the future, at the second coming of Christ. But the association of the lamb with Mount Zion may be purely symbolic. Traditionally, Mount Zion symbolized the presence of God, especially after it was identified with the temple mount. So, the lamb's standing on Mount Zion shows that he is God's agent, just as the beast's rising out of the sea implies that he is an agent of chaos and destruction.

With the Lamb are *a hundred and forty-four thousand who had his name and his Father's name written on their foreheads.* The number calls to mind the 144,000 who are sealed on the forehead (7:1-8). The names written on their foreheads recall the promise to the conquerors in the message to Philadelphia, "I will write on him the name of my God . . . and my own new name" (3:12).

Beginning with vs. 2, the scene shifts to heaven. The 144,000 *sing a new song before the throne* (vs.3). A *new song* was sung by the four living creatures and the twenty-four elders, when the Lamb took the scroll with seven seals from the hand of the enthroned one (5:9). In chapter 5, the new song is quoted. Here, the reader is not told what the words of the song are. The silence on that score gives the impression that the 144,000 is an exclusive group. That impression is reinforced by the remark that *(n)o one could learn that song except the hundred and forty-four thousand who had been redeemed from the earth.*

The following verses imply that the 144,000 are indeed a special group, probably limited to those who die for their faith. Such a death would mean following *the Lamb wherever he goes* in the fullest sense. It would also justify the image *first fruits for God and the Lamb.* This phrase implies that they are offered to God and the Lamb as a sacrifice. They seem to be described here as a special group which achieves perfection—*and in their mouth no lie was found, for they are spotless.*

The 144,000 are those *who have not defiled themselves with women for they are chaste* (literally, "virgins"). Some commentators interpret this statement metaphorically, arguing that the sexual language here is analogous to that found in 2:14 and in chapter 17. Such an interpretation is possible, but the very concrete language used here makes it more likely that actual sexual practice is meant. Even though there is no other reference to sexual abstinence in the Apocalypse, it is likely that this vision advocates it as a mark of the true Christian. Such views were rather common in the early Church, especially in the East. In the Apocalypse, the approval of celibacy may have been inspired by the Israelite traditions of holy war and priesthood. Fighting in holy battle and serving as priest both required temporary sexual abstinence. In the Apocalypse, imagery from both these traditions is used to interpet christian life. The struggle with Rome is interpreted as a holy war. All Christians are priests to God. So celibacy may have been encouraged by John as a symbolic expression of worthiness to participate in christian life so defined.

Since traditionally only males were warriors and priests, John's exclusively male point of view in vs. 4 would be intelligible, if these were the sources of the image. The wording does not necessarily imply that only men were considered christian or expected to be celibate.

Now it is obvious that this vision presents a very stark model of ideal christianity, involving not only celibacy but voluntary, violent death. The wording of the vision implies that it is not an ideal which all Christians are expected to fulfill. It is only for some. Since it is an ideal, those who fulfill it are especially honored. This stark model arises naturally from an apocalyptic mentality, which views the present situation in extreme terms. The conflict is universal and a life and death matter. Life as it has been known is passing away. The world is corrupt and must be destroyed. Celibacy and voluntary death are intelligible responses of the individual Christian in such a framework. According to the vision of the souls under the altar (6:9-11), each voluntary death for the sake of the faith helps bring about the end of the corrupt order and the great renewal. This is not a vision of the ideally christian for all seasons. Only when an apocalyptic view of reality is appropriate are such sacrifices called for.

In the first three visions of this cycle, the emphasis is on the threat which the faithful face. This threat is described in various figurative ways—the dragon's attack on the woman, the first beast making war on the saints, and the second beast causing the deaths of those who refuse to worship the first beast. In this, the fourth vision of the cycle, those stories of threat are balanced by a vision of triumph. Those who conquer are portrayed sharing the Lamb's glory. The intended effect is to encourage the faithful in their commitment to witness to the truth.

A PREVIEW OF THE END:
THE THREE ANGELS.
14:6-13.

⁶Then I saw another angel flying in midheaven, with an eternal gospel to proclaim to those who dwell on earth, to every nation and tribe and tongue and people; ⁷and he said with a loud voice, "Fear God and give him glory, for the hour of his judgment has come; and worship him who made heaven and earth, the sea and the fountains of water."

⁸Another angel, a second, followed, saying, "Fallen, fallen is Babylon the great, she who made all nations drink the wine of her impure passion."

⁹And another angel, a third, followed them, saying with a loud voice, "If any one worships the beast and its image, and receives a mark on his forehead or on his hand, ¹⁰he also shall drink the wine of God's wrath, poured unmixed into the cup of his anger, and he shall be tormented with fire and brimstone in the presence of the holy angels and in the presence of the Lamb. ¹¹And the smoke of their torment goes up for ever and ever; and they have no rest, day or night, these worshipers of the beast and its image, and whoever receives the mark of its name."

¹²Here is a call for the endurance of the saints, those who keep the commandments of God and the faith of Jesus.

> [13]And I heard a voice from heaven saying, "Write this: Blessed are the dead who die in the Lord henceforth." "Blessed indeed," says the Spirit, "that they may rest from their labors, for their deeds follow them!"

This is a vision of three angels, each with a message; the vision is followed by a voice from heaven (vs.13). This vision, with the saying from heaven which follows, provides a preview of the story of the end as it will be narrated in the next two cycles of visions.

The message of the first angel is an eternal gospel which asks all people to *(f)ear God and give him glory, for the hour of his judgment has come.* This proclamation is essentially a call for conversion which might serve as a summary of early christian preaching. The call to worship the maker of the cosmos is a call away from allegiance to the creature and toward allegiance to the creator. The announcement of impending *judgment* prepares for the message of the second angel.

The second angel delivers an oracle reminiscent of older oracles of Isaiah and Jeremiah, *Fallen, fallen is Babylon the great* . . . (Is 21:9, Jer 51:8). John's readers would understand the oracle to refer to the new Babylon, Rome. Rome has become "Babylon," because it was the second great power to destroy Jerusalem and the temple. This brief and powerful announcement is a preview, really only a hint, of what will be told in greater detail in the next cycle.

The message of the third angel continues themes introduced in the earlier visions of this cycle: *If any one worhips the beast* (compare 13:4,8,12) *and its image* (compare 13:15), *and receives a mark on his forehead or on his hand* . . . (compare 13:16). The punishment of those who do these things is announced in the third angel's message. First, it is announced metaphorically, *he also shall drink the wine of God's wrath* . . . . Then their punishment is described in the same way as that of all the wicked in the final cycle of visions—*he shall be tormented with fire and sulphur in the presence of the holy angels and in the presence of the Lamb* . . . (compare 19:20; 20:10,14-15).

Many readers have been offended at what they perceive here as gloating over the prospective torture of the enemies of John and his earliest readers. The function of the passage does not seem to be to give such psychological satisfaction. Rather, the prediction of punishment serves as a threat directed to the faithful to strengthen them in their resistance. What follows supports this interpretation: *Here is a call for the endurance of the saints* . . . . Endurance is encouraged by the threat which which precedes (vss.9-11) and by the promise which follows—*Blessed are the dead who die in the Lord henceforth . . . for their deeds follow them* (vs.13).

The messages of the three angels still speak today. The call to "Fear God" calls us to recognize the limited and relative character of our views. It also challenges us to recognize the fragility of our existence and its character as gift. The announcement of the "hour of judgment" reminds us that we are accountable for our deeds, however the accounting may take place. The invitation to worship the creator involves a deep reverence for the invisible origin of all things and warns against an unbalanced attachment to any of its particular transient manifestations.

"Babylon" is an image for counterfeit power, like the beast from the sea. The oracle of her doom expresses the futility of the will to power which she represents. The threat announced by the third angel implies that those who allow themselves to be seduced by counterfeit power will perish— that such power ultimately destroys those who exercise or submit to it. The blessing called out by the voice from heaven speaks of those *who die in the Lord.* These are they who resist the will to power and are faithful to the source of all things. For them death is rest; it can be accepted as the limit which is set for humanity by providence.

THE DAY OF JUDGMENT.
14:14-20.

> [14]Then I looked, and lo, a white cloud, and seated on the cloud one like a son of man, with a golden crown on his head, and a sharp sickle in his hand. [15]And another

angel came out of the temple, calling with a loud voice to him who sat upon the cloud, "Put in your sickle, and reap, for the hour to reap has come, for the harvest of the earth is fully ripe." [16]So he who sat upon the cloud swung his sickle on the earth, and the earth was reaped.

[17]And another angel came out of the temple in heaven, and he too had a sharp sickle. [18]Then another angel came out from the altar, the angel who has power over fire, and he called with a loud voice to him who had the sharp sickle, "Put in your sickle, and gather the clusters of the vine of the earth, for its grapes are ripe." [19]So the angel swung his sickle on the earth and gathered the vintage of the earth, and threw it into the great wine press of the wrath of God; [20]and the wine press was trodden outside the city, and blood flowed from the wine press, as high as a horse's bridle, for one thousand six hundred stadia.

The vision of the dragon's attack, the first vision in this cycle, places the persecution faced by the earliest readers of the Apocalypse in the framework of a cosmic conflict (chapter 12). The visions of the two beasts further characterize this conflict. As we have noted before, each cycle in the Apocalypse tells the same story of the end which involves (1) persecution, (2) punishment of the nations or judgment, and (3) triumph of God, the Lamb and his followers or salvation. The first three visions of this cycle express the element of persecution. The vision of the 144,000 on Mount Zion with the Lamb is a preliminary vision of salvation. The vision of the three angels, the fifth in the cycle, is primarily a vision of judgment, though salvation is alluded to as well.

This, the sixth vision in the cycle, alludes, in a veiled and fragmentary way, to the final defeat of the nations. This final battle which is their downfall is presented as divine judgment. The sixth seal and the sixth trumpet also refer to divine punishment of the nations.

John sees *a white cloud, and seated on the cloud one like a son of man* . . . . As in the opening vision, "son of man" is not used as a title, as it is in the gospels. Here, the phrase is descriptive, as it is in Daniel. It refers to one in human form, but who is more than human. The following remark, that *another* angel came out of the temple, implies that the one like a son of man is an angel and not Christ. But any one who has read the opening vision would inevitably think of Christ's second coming as Judge when reading this vision.

The command given to the one like a son of man, *Put in your sickle, and reap, for the hour to reap has come, for the harvest of the earth is fully ripe,* calls to mind one of the oracles of the prophet Joel (3:13). There the harvest is a metaphor for the final battle of God against the nations. Here, the harvest of the earth has the same meaning. This interpretation is supported by what follows. Like the oracle in Joel, this vision uses two different metaphors side by side to refer to the same reality, divine judgment of the nations. In both cases, Joel and the Apocalypse, the two images are harvest and vintage.

The application of the images is more clear in the second part of the vision, the description of the vintage (vss. 17-20). The phrase *the great wine press of the wrath of God* recalls the powerful poem on divine vengeance in Is 63:1-6. The mention of God's *wrath* points beyond the image of the vintage to its application, vengeance. The vision becomes even more concrete about its application. As the wine press was trodden, *blood flowed from the wine press, as high as a horse's bridle* . . . . The mention of *blood* and *a horse's bridle* makes clear that the vintage is an image for battle. We noted the same sort of intrusion of military imagery into the visions of the fifth and sixth trumpets. The image of the wine press for the wrath of God is used again in the description of the great battle between Christ and the beast (19:15). It is likely that this vision is a foreshadowing of the one in chapter 19.

In the message of the third angel in the previous vision, judgment was proclaimed against individuals who succumbed to the claims of the beast. There, judgment was a matter of individual choices and their consequences. Here, judgment is described also, but against the whole earth.

One is invited here to think of human communities, institutions and nations and their accountability. This vision expresses confidence in divine justice vis-a-vis these human communities.

THE FAITHFUL TRIUMPH.
15:1-4.

15 Then I saw another portent in heaven, great and wonderful, seven angels with seven plagues, which are the last, for with them the wrath of God is ended.

²And I saw what appeared to be a sea of glass mingled with fire, and those who had conquered the beast and its image and the number of its name, standing beside the sea of glass with harps of God in their hands. ³And they sing the song of Moses, the servant of God, and the song of the Lamb, saying,

"Great and wonderful are thy deeds,
O Lord God the Almighty!
Just and true are thy ways,
O King of the ages!
⁴Who shall not fear and glorify thy name, O Lord!
For thou alone art holy.
All nations shall come and worship thee,
for thy judgments have been revealed."

Like the vision of the seventh seal, this, the seventh vision in the first unnumbered cycle serves as a transition from the unnumbered cycle (12:1 - 15:4) to the seven bowls (15:5 - 19:10). Both of these climactic visions have more than one element. Here, John sees first of all *seven angels with seven plagues* (15:1). Likewise, one of the effects of the opening of the seventh seal was the appearance of seven angels with seven trumpets. Rather than moving immediately to a description of the bowls, however, John describes a vision of the faithful (15:2-4). Similarly, the vision of the angel with a censer postponed the blowing of the trumpets (8:3-5).

The *sea of glass* beside which the conquerors are standing recalls the "sea of glass, like crystal" before the throne in heaven (4:6). The presence of this sea indicates that this is also a heavenly scene and that the conquerors are in the presence of God. This, the seventh vision in the cycle, expresses the third element of the basic story of the Apocalypse—salvation. As in 7:9-17 and 11:15-19, salvation is expressed in terms of heavenly worship.

The hymn in vss. 3-4, taken as a whole, praises God's justice. From the point of view of John and his earliest readers, this divine justice is praised in spite of the circumstances which call it into question. The vision of the 144,000 with the Lamb depicted salvation primarily from an individual's point of view. Here, salvation is described in terms of universal human justice.

This vision serves as a climax to the preceding cycle and also prepares for the following one, the bowls. The conquerors are victorious over the threat of persecution elaborated in chapter 13—they *conquered the beast and its image and the number of its name*. The song which they sing celebrates the revelation of God's judgments, which were announced in the vision of the three angels (14:6-13) and described in the vision of harvest and vintage (14:14-20). The allusion to God's judgments also prepares the way for the divine punishments associated with the seven bowls which follow.

B. FALLEN, FALLEN IS BABYLON THE GREAT!
15:5-19:10.

EACH OF THE CYCLES of visions in the Apocalypse tells the story of the end of the world from a different perspective. In relation to the first half of the book, the cycles of the second half tell the story in greater narrative detail. But the perspectives of the three cycles of part two parallel those of part one. The first unnumbered cycle, like the seven messages, tells the story primarily from the point of view of individuals as members of the community of the Church. The focus there is on the persecution the faithful face, and on defining the nature and origin of the persecution.

Like the cycle of the seven seals, the cycle of the seven bowls (15:5-19:10) tells the story with a somewhat wider horizon. Both cycles emphasize the perspective of humanity as a whole. In both cases, the question of justice is central.

The seven bowls introduce the same story told by the first unnumbered cycle of 12:1-15:4. The link between the two is a literary device to provide the opportunity for telling the story from another point of view. The seven bowls should not be considered to follow chronologically upon the previous visions. Much of the cycle of the seven bowls is an elaboration of what was already announced in the message of the second angel—"Fallen, fallen is Babylon the great, she who made all nations drink the wine of her impure passion" (14:8). The purpose of this cycle is to portray God's justice in a symbolic way.

THE WRATH OF GOD:
THE FIRST FOUR BOWLS.
15:5-16:9.

[5]After this I looked, and the temple of the tent of witness in heaven was opened, [6]and out of the temple came the seven angels with the seven plagues, robed in pure bright linen, and their breasts girded with golden girdles. [7]And one of the four living creatures gave the seven angels seven golden bowls full of the wrath of God who lives for ever and ever; [8]and the temple was filled with smoke from the glory of God and from his power, and no one could enter the temple until the seven plagues of the seven angels were ended.

16 Then I heard a loud voice from the temple telling the seven angels, "Go and pour out on the earth the seven bowls of the wrath of God."

[2]So the first angel went and poured his bowl on the earth, and foul and evil sores came upon the men who bore the mark of the beast and worshiped its image.

[3]The second angel poured his bowl into the sea, and it became like the blood of a dead man, and every living thing died that was in the sea.

[4]The third angel poured his bowl into the rivers and the fountains of water, and they became blood. [5]And I heard the angel of water say,

"Just art thou in these thy judgments,
thou who are and wast, O Holy One.
[6]For men have shed the blood of saints and prophets,
and thou hast given them blood to drink.
[7]And I heard the altar cry,
"Yea, Lord God the Almighty,
true and just are thy judgments!"

[8]The fourth angel poured his bowl on the sun, and it was allowed to scorch men with fire; [9]men were scorched by the fierce heat, and they cursed the name of God who had power over these plagues, and they did not repent and give him glory.

The imagery of the bowls seems to have a dual source; it appears to be a fusion of two elements from the Hebrew Bible. One is the cult of the temple and its vessels. According to Ex 27:3, the priests used bronze basins to carry away the fat and ashes from the sacrifices. Here the angels who empty the bowls upon the world come *out of the temple* in heaven. So the imagery of the bowls is taken from the earthly temple cult and transformed to describe a heavenly ritual with cosmic effects. This heavenly ritual is analogous to the one described in 8:3-5—"the angel took the censer and filled it with fire from the altar and threw it on the earth." In both cases, a heavenly ritual symbolizes the execution of divine wrath upon the earth and its inhabitants.

The other source of the imagery of the bowls is the metaphor of a cup of wine as the wrath of God (see Ps 75:8 and Is 51:17,22). The closest parallel to the use of the metaphor in the Apocalypse is a passage in Jeremiah. The Lord commands the prophet to "take from my hand this cup of wine of wrath, and make all the nations to whom I send you drink it. They shall drink and stagger and be crazed because of the sword which I am sending among them." Jeremiah took the cup and made all the nations drink it: beginning with Jerusalem and the cities of Judah; on to Egypt, Uz and Athens, "all the kingdoms of the world which are on the face of the earth. And after them the king of Babylon shall drink" (Jer 25:15-26). In the introduction to the bowls, they are explicitly associated with "the wrath of God" (15:1). This theme is repeated just before the bowls are poured, *Go and pour out on the earth the seven bowls of the wrath of God* (16:1).

Like the seven trumpets, the seven bowls call to mind the plagues on the Egyptians in the exodus story. The association is encouraged by the introduction to the bowls—John sees seven angels with *seven plagues*. The result of the pouring of the first bowl is that *foul and evil sores came upon the men who bore the mark of the beast and worshiped its image*. This plague is similar to the sixth against the Egyptians: festering boils on human beings and beasts (Ex 9:8-12).

When the second bowl is poured out, the sea *became like the blood of a dead man, and every living thing died that was in the sea. The third angel poured his bowl into the rivers and fountains of water and they became blood.* These two plagues are analogous to the first worked through Moses on the Egyptians—the Nile and all the waters of Egypt turned to blood (Ex 7:14-24).

The story of the exodus is a model for understanding the present situation. God is a God who judges those who unjustly persecute the people of God. As with the trumpets, all humanity is affected by the wrath of God. The reason for the punishment was not expressed in the trumpet cycle. A hint is given by the remark that those who lacked the seal of God are to suffer (9:4). Here, it becomes clear that the plagues are directed against those who gave allegiance to the beast (16:2) and those *who have shed the blood of saints and prophets* (16:6). The implication is that all who do not actively resist the beast are its accomplices.

In keeping with the character of the second half of the book, the bowls manifest an escalation in relation to the trumpets. The trumpets are allowed to affect one-third of humanity. The bowls' effect is total, *for with them the wrath of God is ended* (15:1). Once again, we must remember that the language of the Apocalypse is symbolic. The bowls do not describe events which follow and complete the events of the trumpets. Rather, the visions of the bowls express more fully the absolute accountability of humanity, its thorough-going subjection to the divine forces of judgment.

The first four bowls express the universal and absolute character of divine judgment. They are poured out upon *the earth, the sea, the rivers and the fountains of water*, and upon *the sun*. These elements symbolize the entire cosmos in four major aspects—heaven and earth, salt and fresh waters. Human accountability is related to our status as creatures; it is the Creator who is Judge.

A new element in the bowls in comparison with the trumpets is the interpretation given the third bowl, which causes the rivers and fountains to turn to blood. The interpretation is given in the form of praise offered to God by an angel and by the altar. The saying of the angel proclaims God's justice, like the song of the faithful in 15:3-4. Once again, from the point of view of John and his earliest readers, this affirmation of God's just dealings was made in spite of circumstances which implied the contrary.

A striking characteristic of the angel's saying is the way offense and punishment are correlated—those who *shed the blood of saints and prophets* are given *blood to drink*. This correlation is traditional in Jewish law: "Whoever sheds the blood of man, by man shall his blood be shed . . ." (Gen 9:6). An exact correlation in the angel's saying would call for a punishment by shedding blood, not by giving to drink. The variation is due to the use of the metaphor of "drinking blood" for bloodshed. The same metaphor is used in Apoc 17:6, 18:24. It may have been inspired by Is 49:26.

The mention of the altar in vs. 7 recalls the vision of the souls under the altar following the fifth seal (6:9-11) and the angel taking fire from the altar and casting it upon the earth (8:3-5). These associations imply that the plagues of the seven bowls are divine punishments for the injustices committed against the faithful. This vision expresses in a symbolic way the conviction that the cosmos is truly conditioned by justice, even though its workings are not always apparent.

The story of the third bowl presupposes a certain solidarity between human behavior and the natural world. The murder of the saints is a human sin, but somehow the earth shares responsibility for the sin. So the punishment involves the natural world as well as human life. The story implies, rightly, that the two cannot be separated. Similar ideas are expressed in Gen 3:17 and Is 24:5-6.

The first four bowls express the paradoxical relationship between humanity and nature. The results of human attitudes and deeds are reflected in the natural world. Thus, humanity, in a certain sense, has dominion over nature. On the other hand, humanity's control over nature is not complete. There are both creative and destructive powers in nature which are beyond human control.

IT IS DONE!
THE LAST THREE BOWLS.
16:10-21.

[10]The fifth angel poured his bowl on the throne of the beast, and its kingdom was in darkness; men gnawed their tongues in anguish [11]and cursed the God of heaven for their pain and sores, and did not repent of their deeds.

[12]The sixth angel poured his bowl on the great river Euphrates, and its water was dried up, to prepare the way for the kings from the east. [13]And I saw, issuing from the mouth of the dragon and from the mouth of the beast and from the mouth of the false prophet, three foul spirits like frogs; [14]for they are demonic spirits, performing signs, who go abroad to the kings of the whole world, to assemble them for battle on the great day of God the Almighty. [15]("Lo, I am coming like a thief! Blessed is he who is awake, keeping his garments that he may not go naked and be seen exposed!") [16]And they assembled them at the place which is called in Hebrew Armageddon.

[17]The seventh angel poured his bowl into the air, and a great voice came out of the temple, from the throne, saying, "It is done!" [18]And there were flashes of lightning, loud noises, peals of thunder, and a great earthquake such as had never been since men were on the earth, so great was that earthquake. [19]The great city was split into three parts, and the cities of the nations fell, and God remembered great Babylon, to make her drain the cup of the fury of his wrath. [20]And every island fled away, and no mountains were to be found; [21]and great hailstones, heavy as a hundred-weight, dropped on men from heaven, till men cursed God for the plague of the hail, so fearful was that plague.

The first four bowls are poured out on four major portions of the world which together symbolize the whole cosmos. The fifth bowl is poured out *on the throne of the beast*, showing that the plagues are especially directed against Rome and its collaborators. The *darkness* which follows is reminiscent of the ninth Egyptian plague, "thick darkness in all the land of Egypt" (Ex 10:21-29).

The plague following the fifth bowl does not lead people to repentance. A similar remark follows the sixth trumpet (9:20-21). In the earlier passage, there is no indication that people recognize the divine origin of their anguish. Here, it is implied that they do. But this recognition does not lead to repentance; rather they *cursed the God of heaven for their pain and sores*. This reaction implies an insurmountable alienation between a certain portion of humanity and their creator.

The *three foul spirits like frogs* associated with the sixth bowl recall the second plague against the Egyptians, a swarm of frogs (Ex 7:25-8:15). At the same time, the pouring out of the sixth bowl on *the great river Euphrates* recalls the sixth trumpet (9:13-21), which results in the release of four angels bound at "the great river Euphrates." The Euphrates brings to mind the great empires of the east, especially the Parthians. This impression is reinforced by the remark that the river *was dried up, to prepare the way for the kings from the east*. In the vision of the sixth trumpet, military imagery is combined with descriptions of angelic-demonic beings. There it is not clear how the armies relate to the angels who are to kill a third of humanity. Here the *demonic spirits*, the three foul spirits like frogs, assemble *the kings of the whole world . . . for battle on the great day of God the Almighty*. The vision of the sixth trumpet then seems to be a dream-like preview of the sixth bowl. What the sixth trumpet alludes to in a veiled and fragmentary way, the sixth bowl describes in a more straightforward narrative form. As noted earlier, the first seal alludes to a great battle between the Parthians and Rome. Thus, the first seal, the sixth trumpet and the sixth bowl all allude to the same great military crisis.

The association of the demonic spirits and the kings of the world with the dragon and the two beasts of chapter 13 implies that this great battle is the same one described in 19:11-21 between Christ and the beasts. Thus the military crisis of the sixth bowl is the turning point, the final judgment. This conclusion is reinforced by the saying which follows, *"Lo, I am coming like a thief! Blessed is he who is awake, keeping his garments that he may not go naked and be seen exposed!"* John suddenly steps out of his role as storyteller to address his readers directly. Being ready to face the Lord's judgment is more important than knowing in detail how it will be administered. John returns to his story in vs. 16, saying that the armies assembled *at the place which is called in Hebrew Armageddon.* The story is left unfinished, to be taken up again later.

The name *Armageddon* probably means "the mountain of Megiddo." This powerful passage has made it a symbol of world-wide crisis and judgment for the readers of the Apocalypse and for subsequent generations.

The seventh bowl, on one level of meaning, calls to mind the plagues of Egyptians, as most of the earlier bowls do. The *great hailstones, heavy as a hundred-weight*, allude to the seventh plague on Egypt (Ex 9:13-35), the plague of hail.

The vision of the seventh bowl has two elements; one of these, the plague of hail, continues a major theme of the bowls—that God is still one who judges the enemies of the people of God, as the Egyptians of old were judged. The other element is the fall of Babylon, a theme introduced in the previous cycle in the vision of the three angels (14:8). The image of the beast and the image "Babylon" have not yet been related to one another explicitly. Yet, since both symbolize the Roman empire, the reader has already made the association. The bowls are directed against the beast and its followers (16:2, 6 [indirectly], 10, 13). So the fall of Babylon in the seventh bowl concludes another major theme of the bowls—the conflict of God and his followers with Rome.

In the vision of the seventh bowl, the fall of Babylon is announced summarily. We are told, *It is done!*, before we know what is happening. Suspense is built up with the narration of a tremendous theophany; the *flashes of lightning, voices, peals of thunder* and the *great earthquake* express the active presence of God. Finally the announcement is made *the great city was split into three parts.* Here, the fall of Babylon is figuratively described as the result of a great earthquake. The final battle which signals the end is meant; the remark that *the cities of the nations fell* shows that the final, divine judgment of the nations is the context of Rome's fall.

Babylon's fall is also described as her draining *the cup of the fury of his* (God's) *wrath.* This image of God's wrath as intoxicating wine climaxes the series of bowls whose contents symbolize the wrath of God. This saying creates a contrast with the message of the second angel: "Babylon . . . made all nations drink the wind of her impure passion" (14:8).

The fall of Babylon was originally announced in the vision of the three angels in the briefest way (14:8). The seventh bowl repeats and elaborates that announcement using the images of a destroying earthquake and the cup of God's wrath. The description of the fall of Babylon in the seventh bowl is still veiled and fragmentary. The Babylon appendix (17:1-19:10) at last gives a fuller picture. Thus, the vision of the seventh bowl is transitional, like the vision of the conquerors in 15:2-4. It climaxes the series of the bowls and prepares for the Babylon appendix which follows.

THE BEAST TURNS AGAINST HIS ALLY, THE HARLOT.
17.

17 Then one of the seven angels who had the seven bowls came and said to me, "Come, I will show you the judgment of the great harlot who is seated upon many waters, ²with whom the kings of the earth have committed fornication, and with the wine of whose fornication the dwellers on earth have become drunk." ³And he carried me away in the Spirit into a wilderness, and I saw a woman sitting on a scarlet beast which was full of blasphemous names, and it had seven heads and ten horns. ⁴The woman was arrayed in purple and scarlet, and bedecked with gold and jewels and pearls, holding in her hand a golden cup full of abominations and the impurities of her fornication; ⁵and on her forehead was written a name of mystery: "Babylon the great, mother of harlots and of earth's abominations." ⁶And I saw the woman, drunk with the blood of the saints and the blood of the martyrs of Jesus.

When I saw her I marveled greatly. ⁷But the angel said to me, "Why marvel? I will tell you the mystery of the woman, and of the beast with seven heads and ten horns that carries her. ⁸The beast that you saw was, and is not, and is to ascend from the bottomless pit and go to perdition; and the dwellers on earth whose names have not been written in the book of life from the foundation of the world, will marvel to behold the beast, because it was and is not and is to come. ⁹This calls for a mind with wisdom: the seven heads are seven hills on which the woman is seated; ¹⁰they are also seven kings, five of whom have fallen, one is, the other has not yet come, and when he comes he must remain only a little while. ¹¹As for the beast that was and is not, it is an eighth but it belongs to the seven, and it goes to perdition. ¹²And the ten horns that you saw are ten kings who have not yet received royal power, but they are to receive authority as kings for one hour, together with the beast, ¹³These are of one mind and give over their power and authority to the beast; ¹⁴they will make war on the Lamb, and the Lamb will conquer them, for he is Lord of lords and King of kings, and those with him are called and chosen and faithful."

¹⁵And he said to me, "The waters that you saw, where the harlot is seated, are peoples and multitudes and

nations and tongues. [16]And the ten horns that you saw, they and the beast will hate the harlot; they will make her desolate and naked, and devour her flesh and burn her up with fire, [17]for God has put it into their hearts to carry out his purpose by being of one mind and giving over their royal power to the beast, until the words of God shall be fulfilled. [18]And the woman that you saw is the great city which has dominion over the kings of the earth."

Rather than beginning a new version of the story of the end, the Babylon appendix elaborates an aspect of the story as told by the seven bowls. This relationship is shown by the introduction to the appendix; it is *one of the seven angels who had the seven bowls* who shows John the opening vision of the appendix and explains it to him.

The vision of chapter 17 centers on *the great harlot* who symbolizes a city, *Babylon*. The personification of a city as a woman is very common in the Hebrew prophets. Even earlier, it was common for the peoples of the ancient Near East to personify their cities, sometimes as a local goddess of Fortune. The use of a female image was suggested perhaps by the secure, encircling character of a city's walls, which would symbolize the womb or a mother's protective arms. An example of the positive use of the feminine metaphor is "mother Jerusalem" (Is 66:7-14).

The image of a *harlot* for a city which counted as Israel's enemy is also found in the Hebrew prophets. Nahum called Nineveh a harlot "graceful and of deadly charms, who betrays nations with her harlotries and peoples with her charms" (Nahum 3:4). Isaiah applied the image to Tyre — she "will play the harlot with all the kingdoms of the world upon the face of the earth" (Is 23:17). In the Isaiah passage, harlotry is associated with trade (vs. 18). The images of *fornication* and becoming *drunk* here are analogous. They symbolize the way in which the values of imperial Rome pervaded the Mediterranean world. John here condemns these values.

The description of the harlot as *seated upon many waters* is also a motif from the prophets. Jeremiah spoke of Babylon as "you who dwell by many waters" (Jer 51:13). The allusion is to the Euphrates and the many canals surrounding the ancient city of Babylon. The prophet Nahum, in describing the Egyptian city of Thebes, shows that such a location was a sign of strength — "with water around her, her rampart a sea, and water her wall" (Nahum 3:8). The description does not at all fit the historical city of Rome. It is taken over to show that Rome is the new Babylon. A new meaning is given the phrase in vs. 15: the waters are *peoples and multitudes and nations and tongues.* Rome's strength is symbolized by the peoples subject to its rule.

Several other remarks show that "Babylon" is a veiled reference to Rome. The name written on her forehead, *Babylon the great...,* is called *a name of mystery.* The implication is that the name "Babylon" should not be taken at face value. Later, the seven heads are interpreted as *seven mountains on which the woman is seated.* This interpretation alludes to the seven hills of Rome. The vision closes with a final hint — *the woman that you saw is the great city which has dominion over the kings of the earth.* The most obvious candidate for this title in John's time was the mighty, imperial city of Rome.

The clothing of the woman — *purple and scarlet* — symbolizes a life of luxury. Her adornment — *gold and jewels and pearls* — represents the wiles of a woman who wishes to seduce a man who is not her husband.

Throughout the vision, images of harlotry and fornication are used to represent the idea of idolatry. Chapter 13 made clear that Rome's idolatry consisted in its arrogant pride in its accomplishments, its excessive claims of allegiance and praise, and its illusion of complete autonomy. In chapter 13, the emphasis was on the beast's relationship to the creator and to the faithful. Here, Rome's role in the civilization of the Mediterranean world is emphasized. Rome is depicted as a harlot because she seduced many of the local rulers and ordinary people into accepting her illusory and exaggerated view of her own importance.

This vision claims that the beautiful and luxurious facade conceals an insidious and disgusting corruption. She drinks from *a golden cup,* but it contains filth. The true nature of the empire is shown in its ruthless slaughter of the innocent—she is *drunk with the blood of the saints and the blood of the martyrs of Jesus.*

Rome is called *mother of harlots and of earth's abominations.* Surely this is a one-sided view of ancient Rome. John here claims that all the wrongs of the world are due to Rome's influence, that it is the root of all evil. Certainly Rome had moments of true greatness and contributed much to human well-being in its own time and to the development of human civilization. John wrote from an apocalyptic viewpoint which sees reality in black and white terms. Such a view has little appreciation for the shades of gray. The Apocalypse's bold characterization of Rome did capture the dark side of imperial power which must not be overlooked. But its visions must be taken as hyperbolic stories which make their point in extreme terms. These visions may not, however, be applied literally and simply to particular human beings or institutions without severely distorting reality.

The harlot is sitting on *a scarlet beast which was full of blasphemous names, and it had seven heads and ten horns.* None of the other beasts in the Apocalypse so far has been described as *scarlet,* though the dragon of chapter 12 is red. The blasphemous names, seven heads and ten horns make it similar to the beast from the sea in chapter 13. The reader, like John, is puzzled at first by this vision. The angel explains, *The beast that you saw was, and is not, and is to ascend from the bottomless pit and go to perdition.* This remark is repeated in slightly different form—*it was and is not and is to come.* The angel's explanation alerts the reader that this beast is the same one mentioned in 11:7, "the beast that ascends from the bottomless pit."

The reader still wonders how the beast of chapters 11 and 17 relates to those of chapter 13. It was noted earlier that a being ascending from a bottomless pit is part of the story of cosmic combat for kingship. The rebel is confined to the underworld when partially defeated. His rising from the pit then symbolizes renewed revolt, the resurgence of chaos. The sea, likewise, is associated with the rebel in the combat story. So the beast from the pit and the beast from the sea have the same symbolic function. Thus, the beasts in chapters 11, 13:1-10, and 17 have the same significance. On one level, they express chaos and destruction; on another, they represent the Roman empire, particularly Nero.

During John's time, legends were circulating about Nero, hinting that he would return to regain rule of Rome. These legends stand behind the remark that one of the beast's heads (or the beast himself) had a mortal wound which had healed (13:3,14). The same legends are reflected here in chapter 17 in the statement that the beast was, is not and is to ascend from the bottomless pit. Nero was (he ruled Rome in his lifetime), is not (he is dead at present), and is to ascend (he will return from the realm of the dead as the Antichrist).

This interpretation of the beast in chapter 17 is supported by the explanation of the ten horns (vss.12-14,16-17). They are *ten kings* who will become the beast's allies; together with the beast they will attack and destroy the harlot—*they will make her desolate and naked, and devour her flesh and burn her up with fire.* This part of chapter 17 also refers to the legends about Nero. Some thought that he had taken political asylum with the Parthians and that they would assist him in regaining power over Rome. In the great battle that would follow, however, the city of Rome would be destroyed and the East would dominate the Mediterranean world once again. John apparently expected these predictions to be fulfilled and saw them as God's will—*for God has put it into their hearts to carry out his purpose by being of one mind and giving over their royal power to the beast until the words of God shall be fulfilled.* John also apparently believed that the great battle initiated by Nero and the Parthians against Rome would trigger the final battle of judgment—*they will make war on the Lamb, and the Lamb will conquer them, for he is Lord of lords and King of kings . . . .* The first seal (6:1-2), the sixth trumpet (9:13-21) and the sixth bowl (16:12-16) all are fragmentary and veiled allusions to the attack on Rome led by Nero and the Parthians. The sixth seal (6:12-17), the seventh trumpet (11:15-19) and the vision of one like a son of man (14:14-20) allude to the ultimate battle of the Lamb which was to follow.

John's probable expectations with regard to historical events were not fulfilled. It is unlikely that he considered the emperor Domitian, reigning in John's time, to be the returned Nero. The second explanation of the beast's heads does not support that conclusion; *they are also seven kings, five of whom have fallen, one is, the other has not yet come, and when he comes he must remain only a little while.* The beast *is an eighth but it belongs to the seven.* There is no good reason to doubt that John wrote during the time of the king he said "is"—the sixth. If Domitian were considered the returned Nero, John would have been writing under the eighth king.

The allusion to the seven kings, or emperors, is deliberately vague, The image is flexible, so that, as historical circumstances change, it can be reinterpreted. The power and validity of such prophecies do not depend on their historical accuracy. Their power lies in their striking images and in the dynamic pattern of their stories. These images and stories are powerful because they illuminate more than one particular historical situation. The story of the beast and the ten kings turning against their once favored harlot applies to many situations in which people or groups vying for counterfeit power destroy one another. This story shows one of the inherent flaws of the will to power. It does not unite; it divides.

A DIRGE OVER THE FALLEN CITY.
18.

18   After this I saw another angel coming down from heaven, having great authority; and the earth was made bright with his splendor. [2]And he called out with a mighty voice,

"Fallen, fallen is Babylon the great!
It has become a dwelling place of demons,
a haunt of every foul spirit,
a haunt of every foul and hateful bird;
[3]for all nations have drunk the wine of her impure passion,
and the kings of the earth have committed fornication with her,
and the merchants of the earth have grown rich with the wealth of her wantonness."

[4]Then I heard another voice from heaven saying,

"Come out of her, my people,
lest you take part in her sins,
lest you share in her plagues;
[5]for her sins are heaped high as heaven,
and God has remembered her iniquities/
[6]Render to her as she herself has rendered,
and repay her double for her deeds;
mix a double draught for her in the cup she mixed.
[7]As she glorified herself and played the wanton,
so give her a like measure of torment and mourning.
Since in her heart she says, 'A queen I sit,
I am no widow, mourning I shall never see,'
[8]so shall her plagues come in a single day,
pestilence and mourning and famine,
and she shall be burned with fire;
for mighty is the Lord God who judges her."

[9]And the kings of the earth, who committed fornication and were wanton with her, will weep and wail over her when they see the smoke of her burning; [10]they will stand far off, in fear of her torment, and say,

"Alas! alas! thou great city,
thou mighty city, Babylon!
In one hour has thy judgment come."

[11]And the merchants of the earth weep and mourn for her, since no one buys their cargo any more, [12]cargo of gold, silver, jewels and pearls, fine linen, purple, silk

and scarlet, all kinds of scented wood, all articles of ivory, and articles of costly wood, bronze, iron and marble, [13]cinnamon, spice, incense, myrrh, frankincense, wine, oil, fine flour and wheat, cattle and sheep, horses and chariots, and slaves, that is, human souls.

[14]"The fruit for which they soul longed has gone from thee,

and all thy dainties and thy splendor are lost to thee,
never to be found again!"

[15]The merchants of these wares, who gained wealth from her, will stand far off, in fear of her torment, weeping and mourning aloud,

[16]"Alas, alas, for the great city

that was clothed in fine linen, in purple and scarlet,
bedecked with gold, with jewels, and with pearls!

[17]In one hour all this wealth has been laid waste."

And all shipmasters and seafaring men, sailors and all whose trade is on the sea, stood far off [18]and cried out as they saw the smoke of her burning,

"What city was like the great city?" [19]And they threw dust on their heads, as they wept and mourned, crying out,

"Alas, alas, for the great city

where all who had ships at sea grew rich by her wealth!
In one hour she has been laid waste.

[20]Rejoice over her, O heaven,

O saints and apostles and prophets, for God has
given judgment for you against her!"

[21]Then a mighty angel took up a stone like a great millstone and threw it into the sea, saying,.

"So shall Babylon the great city be thrown down
with violence,

and shall be found no more;

[22]and the sound of harpers and minstrels, of flute players
and trumpeters,

shall be heard in thee no more;

and a craftsman of any craft

shall be found in thee no more;

and the sound of the millstone
shall be heard in thee no more;
²³and the light of a lamp
shall shine in thee no more;
and the voice of bridegroom and bride
shall be heard in thee no more;
for thy merchants were the great men of the earth,
and all nations were deceived by thy sorcery.
²⁴And in her was found the blood of prophets and of saints,
and of all who have been slain on earth."

Chapter 18 is quite different in form from chapter 17. Chapter 18 deals with the destruction of the city of Rome, which is called "Babylon." But the actual destruction of the city is not seen in a vision or described directly by John. This chapter is rather like an act of a play which focuses on a great battle or some other violent disaster. The violent scene takes place offstage—it is left to the viewer's or reader's imagination. The actual scenes presented on stage show the reactions of the characters in the play to the catastrophe.

John presents six brief scenes which portray various responses to the fall of the great city. The first is a vision of *an angel coming down from heaven, having great authority* (vss.1-3). The second scene consists of an audition; John hears an oracle given by a *voice from heaven* (vss.4-8). The *kings of the earth* appear in the third scene, mourning the city's fall (vss.9-10). The fourth scene consists of the lament over Rome by *merchants of the earth* (vss.11-17a). The *shipmasters and seafaring men, sailors and all whose trade is on the sea* express their dismay in the fifth scene (vss.17b-19). The chapter closes, as it began, with a vision of an angel (vss.21-23). Two isolated sayings also appear, one after the fifth scene (vs.20) and one at the very end (vs.24).

John does not show any great interest in chronology, in any logical sequence of tenses, in this chapter. In the first scene, the angel announces Rome's fall as an event of the past: *Fallen, fallen is Babylon the great! It has become a dwelling place of demons* .... The oracle of the second scene is a warning addressed to God's people just *prior* to the city's destruction—*so shall her plagues come in a single day ... and she shall be burned with fire.* The fourth scene is future and the fifth shifts from the present (vs.11) to the future (vs.15). The sixth scene is set in the past—*all shipmasters ... stood far off and cried out* .... Like the opening scene, it presupposes the fall of Rome. The closing scene is future, but the last saying (vs.24) is in the past tense: *And in her was found the blood of prophets and of saints* ....

The variation in tense is due partly to the literary form of narrative—John is relating what he *saw* and *heard*; the past tense is a function of the story form. On the other hand, the story is about the future. So the tension between form and content explains the vacillation in tense to some extent. The lack of consistency, however, shows that John was not particularly concerned with chronology. His primary intention was not to provide the readers with a detailed guide to the future, but to influence how they understood the present time and how they would act now in preparation for events expected in the near future.

The description of the wasted city in the first scene (vss. 1-3) was inspired by various oracles in the books of Isaiah and Jeremiah against cities which were Israel's enemies, especially Babylon. The root image is a destruction so total that no rebuilding is even attempted. Abandoned totally by people, the city is inhabited only by wild animals of particularly eerie sorts. The place then takes on a haunted character and people suppose that demons and unclean spirits have taken over the site (see Is 13:19-22, 34:8-17, Jer 51:36-37).

In the vision of the harlot, the "fornication" of the kings of the earth and the dwellers on earth refers at least in part to the concern for trade and wealth stimulated by the Roman empire. Here this association is made more explicit. Becoming drunk with her and fornicating with her is synonymous with growing *rich with the wealth of her wantonness.* The *merchants* mentioned here are wholesalers who suddenly became very wealthy toward the end of the first century A.D. by providing for the city of Rome and the army, through trade with the Far East and Africa, and by trade among the provinces. At first the goods involved were necessities, but as prosperity grew, more luxurious items were considered necessities by the middle class— colored cloth and spices, for example. The condemnation of this activity here calls to mind the black horse whose rider had a balance in his hand (the third seal, 6:5-6). That vision reflects a situation in which luxury items are plentiful and cheap, but the necessities are expensive and scarce. The wholesalers' interest in profits is held responsible for the experience of hard times by the poor.

In the second scene (vss. 4-8), a heavenly voice calls, *Come out of her, my people.* This saying was probably inspired by similar oracles in Jeremiah (50:8; 51:6,45). In the Apocalypse, it may be intended literally as a warning to Christians living in the city of Rome. It is more likely that the command is metaphorical and calls for resistance to the values and life-style typical of Roman civilization. If so, then this saying is similar in purpose to the exhortations in the messages to Ephesus, Pergamum and Thyatira which condemn an easy accommodation to the current cultural mores.

The same voice cries, *Render to her as she herself has rendered, and repay her double for her deeds.* Rome is to be destroyed as she destroyed other cities. The allusion is to the wars waged by Rome for control over the other peoples of the Mediterranean world, especially the destruction of Jerusalem in 70 A.D.

The last element in the second scene is a condemnation of Rome's false sense of security. This illusory security is described in terms reminiscent of Is 47:7-10. John, in agreement with the earlier prophet, portrays this attitude as blasphemy, as revolt against God. The crucial failing of Rome is her claim of *aeternitas*, the illusory belief that her prosperity and power would endure forever. Such a claim is a fundamental misunderstanding of the fragile and transient character of human life.

The *kings of the earth* in the third scene (vss.9-10) probably refers to the minor kings whose rule was dependent on Roman favor; there were several such monarchs in Asia Minor in John's time. The *fornication* and wantonness of which they are accused is the same as that mentioned in vs. 3—a love of luxury which, in effect, robs from the poor. That her judgment came in *one hour* recalls the saying in chapter 17, that the ten kings (not the same group as the *kings of the earth*) would receive authority as kings for "one hour." They are allowed this royal rule in order to destroy Rome (17:12-13,16-17).

The fourth scene (vss.11-17a) portrays the mourning of *the merchants of the earth*, the wholesalers who have profited by Roman trade. The list of items in their cargo ends with the word "and bodies and souls of human beings" (translating literally from the Greek). The Greek word for "bodies" was often used to mean "slaves." The last item, "souls of human beings," may be an explanatory addition, another way of saying "slaves." Perhaps John uses both terms to imply that Roman power has taken control not only of the external aspects of many lives, but their internal aspects as well. John does not speak out directly against slavery, but his words imply that human beings should not be bought and sold.

In the fifth scene (vss.17b-19), the *shipmasters and seafaring men, sailors and all whose trade is on the sea* express their grief at the fall of Rome. Their words and actions are very similar to those of the kings and merchants.

After these three scenes of mourning, a call for rejoicing follows abruptly (vs.20). The implication is that Rome's fall is divine punishment for the persecution of *saints, apostles* and *prophets*. This theme is developed further in the saying at the end of the chapter (vs.24). Rome's first crucial sin is that of false security (vss.7-8). The second is the violence done, not only to Christians, but to *all who have been slain on earth* (vs.24).

These two sayings frame the sixth and last scene of the chapter—the vision of the *mighty angel* with a *millstone* (vss.21-23). Throwing the millstone into the sea is a prophetic, symbolic action expressing Rome's fall. It is combined with an oracle of doom (vss.22-23). This scene is similar in tone and content to the opening scene.

This passage seems to support the theory of D. H. Lawrence, that the Apocalypse was written by and for "have-nots" out of spite and envy of the "haves." This theory results from a superficial reading of the text. Two factors are essential for placing this passage in an appropriate perspective.

Both these factors are historical matters. One is that John probably was writing after Roman armies had destroyed Jerusalem in 70 A.D. The other factor is that he knew of Nero's slaughter of Christians in Rome in the 60's. He was also aware of the tendency of Roman officials to execute confessing Christians, following Nero's precedent. Thus John had an extremely different perspective on Roman rule than Paul had when he called for obedience to the authorities (Romans 13). The empire's dark side was all too visible for John.

In this passage Rome is condemned primarily for hubris and murder. The theme of wealth or luxury is also present, but in an ambiguous way. Great wealth evokes both fascination and repulsion. The call, *Come out of her, my people*, implies that at least some of the earliest readers had a share in Roman prosperity. The mourning scenes (vss. 9-19) express at least awe and possibly some sorrow at Rome's downfall. The lists of fine wares are so detailed that they imply a certain admiration for the quality and quantity of Roman trade.

The impression one receives from these scenes of mourning is not one of envy. The passage is not condemning civilization as such. Rather, it calls for an appreciation of the transience of life, the fleeting character of wealth and power—*(i)n one hour all this wealth has been laid waste*. The scenes of mourning remind the readers of the limits which are set to human accomplishments and enjoyments.

THE KINGDOM OF GOD AND THE MARRIAGE SUPPER OF THE LAMB.
19:1-10.

19   After this I heard what seemed to be the mighty voice of a great multitude in heaven, crying,

"Hallelujah! Salvation and glory and power belong to our God,

²for his judgments are true and just;

he has judged the great harlot who corrupted the earth with her fornication,

and he has avenged on her the blood of his servants."

³Once more they cried,

"Hallelujah! The smoke from her goes up for ever and ever."

⁴And the twenty-four elders and the four living creatures fell down and worshiped God who is seated on the throne, saying, "Amen, Hallelujah!" ⁵And from the throne came a voice crying,

"Praise our God, all you his servants,

you who fear him, small and great."

⁶Then I heard what seemed to be the voice of a great multitude, like the sound of many waters and like the sound of mighty thunderpeals, crying,

"Hallelujah! For the Lord our God the Almighty reigns.

⁷Let us rejoice and exult and give him the glory,

for the marriage of the Lamb has come,

and his Bride has made herself ready;

⁸it was granted her to be clothed with fine linen, bright and pure"—

for the fine linen is the righteous deeds of the saints.

⁹And the angel said to me, "Write this: Blessed are those who are invited to the marriage supper of the Lamb." And he said to me, "These are true words of God." ¹⁰Then I fell down at his feet to worship him, but he said to me, "You must not do that! I am a fellow servant with you and your brethren who hold the testimony of Jesus. Worship God." For the testimony of Jesus is the spirit of prophecy.

Chapters 6-22 of the Apocalypse speak about the future. These chapters are organized into five cycles of visions, each of which tells a story with the same basic pattern as the others. Each story involves (1) persecution, (2) punishment of the nations or judgment, and (3) triumph of God, the Lamb and his followers or salvation.

In the cycle of the seven bowls, persecution is emphasized in the vision of the third angel. The rivers and fountains of water are turned into blood because "men have shed the blood of saints and prophets" (16:6). The element of judgment is present in the seventh bowl, which leads to the destruction of "Babylon" (16:19). The punishment of "Babylon," Rome, is elaborated in chapters 17-18.

The climax of the cycle comes in 19:1-10. It is here that the element of triumph or salvation is expressed. The passage opens with an audition: John heard *what seemed to be the loud voice of a great multitude in heaven.* Their first song calls for rejoicing at God's judgment of the harlot, because her downfall is punishment for the murder of the faithful. *Salvation* here probably means "victory"; so the multitude is singing a victory song to celebrate God's triumph over Rome. The language of victory shows that the story of combat is in the background; Rome's rule is seen as rebellion against God, against the created order. The fall of Rome is seen as God's quelling of that revolt.

Cosmic combat is often a struggle for kingship. The victor either becomes king or re-establishes his kingship over the world. So it is here; God's victory over Babylon is a re-establishment of God's rule according to another song of the multitude—*Hallelujah! For the Lord our God the Almighty reigns* (vs.6).

When the rightful king is established in his rule, the forces of chaos and destruction are once more held in check. They no longer flourish, but the world is once again orderly and fertile. The fertility of the new order is expressed here in the image of the *marriage of the Lamb.*

The *Bride* of the Lamb is not simply identified with the Church. Her *fine linen, bright and pure* is explained as *the righteous deeds of the saints.* The explanation shows that the Bride is somehow associated with the church, but not in an abstract, allegorical way. There is no simple, one-to-one correspondence. Rather, the marriage of the Lamb is a metaphor which expresses something about the quality of life determined by God's rule. It is joyful, abundant, life-affirming existence.

The fertility or abundance of the new order is expressed often in a great banquet which follows the victory of the new king. This element is also present here in the *marriage supper of the Lamb* (vs.9). The banquet as an image for the Kingdom of God occurs frequently in the synoptic gospels (for example, Mt 22:1-14 and parallels). In all of these cases, the well-known joy of a feast is used to illuminate the less-known delight of God's rule.

This passage is one of the sources for the later image of the soul as the Bride of Christ. This image was very powerfully employed by J. S. Bach in his cantata, "Wachet Auf" ("Awake"). Here the tenderness, intimacy and companionship of marriage illuminates the spiritual fulfillment which is experienced in union with Christ.

The image of the banquet does not encourage an attitude of "Eat, drink and be merry, for tomorrow we die." Rather, it affirms a continuity between the visible and the invisible. The abundance of food and drink points to the experience of another kind of abundance.

Both images, "marriage" and "banquet," are world-affirming symbols. They celebrate life in the world and affirm the flesh; they imply just the opposite of the symbols of celibacy and voluntary death found in chapter 14. The readers must discern which symbols are appropriate for their particular circumstances.

C. THE DESTINY OF THE WORLD.
19:11 - 22:5.

THE LAST CYCLE of visions in the Apocalypse consists of seven unnumbered visions followed by the Jerusalem appendix (21:9-22:5). It is like the cycle of 12:1-15:5 in that its visions are unnumbered. Its form is similar to the seven bowls in that it has an appendix which elaborates the seventh vision in the series.

This second unnumbered cycle of visions tells the same basic story as the other cycles of the Apocalypse. It differs from the others in that the basic pattern appears twice. Persecution is alluded to for the first time through the mention of "those who had been beheaded for their testimony to Jesus and for the Word of God" (20:4). The judgment of the nations and other enemies of God is described in the visions of battle and punishment in 19:11-20:3. The triumph of Christ and the salvation of those who died for their faith are portrayed in the vision of the thousand year reign (20:4-6).

The element of persecution appears again when Satan is loosed and attacks "the camp of the saints" (20:9). The punishment of Satan (20:10) and the general judgment (20:11-15) follow. Finally, salvation is described in splendid detail (21:1-22:5).

The first cycle in the second half of the Apocalypse (12:1-15:5) tells the story of the end from the point of view of the persecuted individual as a member of the community of the church. The second cycle, the seven bowls, tells the story from the perspective of the struggle between God and

Rome for the allegiance of all humanity. This last cycle of part two, like the last cycle of part one, the trumpets, tells the story from an even broader perspective—from the point of view of the very nature of reality.

THE SECOND COMING OF CHRIST.
19:11-16.

> [11]Then I saw heaven opened, and behold a white horse! He who sat upon it is called Faithful and True, and in righteousness he judges and makes war. [12]His eyes are like a flame of fire, and on his head are many diadems; and he has a name inscribed which no one knows but himself. [13]He is clad in a robe dipped in blood, and the name by which he is called is The Word of God. [14]And the armies of heaven, arrayed in fine linen, white and pure, followed him on white horses. [15]From his mouth issues a sharp sword with which to smite the nations, and he will rule them with a rod of iron; he will tread the wine press of the fury of the wrath of God the Almighty. [16]On his robe and on his thigh he has a name inscribed, King of kings and Lord of lords.

The cyclical character of the Apocalypse is nowhere more apparent than in the transition from 19:1-10 to 19:11-16. The victory of God and the Lamb was celebrated in 19:1-10 and its joyful consequences constitute salvation. All of a sudden in 19:11-16, battle is renewed.

The literary "excuse" for beginning again is that the whole story has not yet been told. In chapter 17, it was implied that after Nero and the Parthians destroyed Rome, the final battle would take place (17:12-14,16-17). The victory songs of 19:1-10 relate primarily to the first battle which leads to Rome's fall. The vision of 19:11-16 relates the second and final battle. So in one sense, 19:11-16 is a new beginning. In another, it recapitulates what has already been told.

In reading this opening vision of the last cycle, one has the impression of returning to the beginning and thus of nearing the end. John *saw heaven opened*. The last time he saw heaven opened was at the beginning of the throne vision (4:1). The rider who appears is called *Faithful and True*. These epithets recall the description of Jesus as "the faithful witness" in the greeting (1:5) and as "the faithful and true witness" in the message to Laodicea (3:14). The horseman is also one who *judges and makes war* in righteousness. The activity of judging calls to mind the presentation of Christ as cosmic judge in John's inaugural vision (1:9-3:22). His making war recalls the threat in the message to Pergamum, ". . . I will come to you soon and war against them with the sword of my mouth" (2:16). The image of the sword appears in this vision also (19:15). The implication is that this last cycle symbolizes the fulfillment of the promises and threats made in the seven messages. This impression is confirmed by further elements linking this vision with the messages: *eyes are like a flame of fire* (1:14,2:18), a special *name* (2:17, 3:12), ruling *with a rod of iron* (2:27).

This vision is a stark and powerful vision of Christ as judge of the world. His portrayal as *The Word of God* with a *sharp sword* issuing from his mouth was probably inspired by a passage in the Wisdom of Solomon, which refers to the night of the first Passover, when all the first-born of Egypt were slain by God's command—"For while gentle silence enveloped all things, and night in its swift course was now half gone, thy all-powerful word leaped from heaven, from the royal throne, into the midst of the land that was doomed, a stern warrior carrying the sharp sword of thy authentic command, and stood and filled all things with death, and touched heaven while standing on the earth" (Wis 18:14-16).

The *robe dipped in blood* and his treading *the wine press of the fury of the wrath of God the Almighty* are allusions to the great poem depicting Yahweh as the Divine Warrior in Is 63:1-6. The implication is that God exercises judgment through Christ. Another motif from the Hebrew bible is the *armies of heaven* who follow Christ. The ancient tradition of holy war is revived here and applied to Christ.

The significance of this vision of Christ as judge is best discussed in connection with the next two visions.

CALL TO A GRISLY BANQUET.
19:17-18.

> [17]Then I saw an angel standing in the sun, and with a loud voice he called to all the birds that fly in mid-heaven, "Come, gather for the great supper of God, [18]to eat the flesh of kings, the flesh of captains, the flesh of mighty men, the flesh of horses and their riders, and the flesh of all men, both free and slave, both small and great."

Next John *saw an angel standing in the sun* who invites *all the birds that fly in mid-heaven* to come to *the great supper of God*. This is quite a different example of the banquet image from the marriage supper of the Lamb (19:9). Here the great banquet consists of a feast for birds on *the flesh of kings, the flesh of captains, the flesh of mighty men, the flesh of horses and their riders, and the flesh of all men* . . . ; that is, on the flesh of the enemies about to be slain by the cosmic judge. This vision was probably inspired by the oracle against Gog and Magog in Ezekiel, where the final battle is followed by a feast for birds and beasts on the flesh of the mighty who have fallen (Ez 39:17-20). In the Ezekiel passage the banquet is called a sacrificial feast—the bodies of the slain are equated with rams, lambs and goats (vs. 18).

A similar equivalence is made in an oracle against the nations in Isaiah between the corpses and blood of the fallen and the fat and blood of sacrificial animals. The Isaiah passage makes clear that this sacrificial banquet has roots in the combat story. Following the victory of the king, fertility is established: ". . . Their land shall be soaked with blood, and their soil made rich with fat" (Is 34:7).

The implications of this vision will be discussed in connection with the following one.

THE FINAL BATTLE.
19:19-21.

> [19]And I saw the beast and the kings of the earth with their armies gathered to make war against him who sits upon the horse and against his army. [20]And the beast was captured, and with it the false prophet who in its presence had worked the signs by which he deceived those who had received the mark of the beast and those who worshiped its image. These two were thrown alive into the lake of fire that burns with brimstone. [21]And the rest were slain by the sword of him who sits upon the horse, the sword that issues from his mouth; and all the birds were gorged with their flesh.

Next John *saw the beast and the kings of the earth with their armies gathered to make war against him who sits upon the horse and against his army.* The beast and his allies are defeated and *thrown alive into the lake of fire that burns with brimstone.* Their punishment shows that, once again, the story of combat is in the background. Often, the victor confines his defeated foe to the earth (as opposed to heaven), in the underworld, at the foot of or under a mountain or volcano. The lake of fire combines the elements of punishment by fire and confinement of a rebellious foe.

Many readers of the Apocalypse are offended by the visions of 19:11-21 because of their apparent bloodthirsty interest in vengeance and violence. Such offense is a misunderstanding of the type of language used here and of its function. One must admit first of all that this passage is not fully compatible with Jesus' teaching to love one's enemies. There is indeed a hope here for the punishment of the wicked. This hope, however, complements Jesus' teaching with an explicit concern for justice in the world which is one of the great contributions of the Jewish heritage.

One must go on to say that the punishment of the wicked, according to 19:11-21, is not in the hands of human beings. If violence is necessary, it is not to be executed by individuals or even by agents of groups. Rather, it is left to providence.

From a broader perspective, this passage implies something about the nature of reality. The values of creation, order, peace and justice are in constant struggle with the values of chaos and destruction. This passage describes the final victory of the forces of creation over those of chaos. This does not necessarily mean that at some point in the future the values of creation will be permanently established and fully eliminate those of chaos. Rather, it implies that the fundamental character of reality is better expressed in order than in chaos, that order, peace and justice are more real and true than their opposites. Therefore, one can assume an attitude of trust in the creator; it is worthwhile aligning oneself and one's efforts with the forces of order, peace and justice.

THE BINDING OF SATAN.
20:1-3.

> **20** Then I saw an angel coming down from heaven, holding in his hand the key of the bottomless pit and a great chain. ²And he seized the dragon, that ancient serpent, who is the Devil and Satan, and bound him for a thousand years, ³and threw him into the pit, and shut it and sealed it over him, that he should deceive the nations no more, till the thousand years were ended. After that he must be loosed for a little while.

The binding of Satan in this vision is parallel to the confinement of the beast and the false prophet to the lake of fire in the previous vision. John is retelling the ancient story of combat to say something about the nature and function of the forces of chaos and evil.

The particular form of this vision recalls the vision of the fifth trumpet. There a star fell from heaven, was given the key of the shaft of the bottomless pit, and opened it, loosing a plague of demonic locusts on the earth. Here John sees *an angel coming down from heaven, holding in his hand the key of the bottomless pit.* He seizes Satan, binds him with a chain and confines him in the pit for a thousand years. Both visions presume stories of combat in which supernatural beings rebel against the universal king, are defeated and are bound and/or confined by the victor.

These stories are figurative or metaphorical and have many meanings and applications. The rebellion implies that creation is never an absolute and final achievement. Chaos is only confined, not destroyed. But the forces of order and creation do have the edge—they are most in tune with reality at its most basic level.

THE THOUSAND YEAR REIGN.
20:4-10.

⁴Then I saw thrones, and seated on them were those to whom judgment was committed. Also I saw the souls of those who had been beheaded for their testimony to Jesus and for the word of God, and who had not worshiped the beast or its image and had not received its mark on their foreheads or their hands. They came to life, and reigned with Christ a thousand years. ⁵The rest of the dead did not come to life until the thousand years were ended. This is the first resurrection. ⁶Blessed and holy is he who shares in the first resurrection! Over such the second death has no power, but they shall be priests of God and of Christ, and they shall reign with him a thousand years.

⁷And when the thousand years are ended, Satan will be loosed from his prison ⁸and will come out to deceive the nations which are at the four corners of the earth, that is, Gog and Magog, to gather them for battle; their number is like the sand of the sea. ⁹And they marched up over the broad earth and surrounded the camp of the saints and the beloved city; but fire came down from heaven and consumed them, ¹⁰and the devil who had deceived them was thrown into the lake of fire and brimstone where the beast and the false prophet were, and they will be tormented day and night for ever and ever.

This vision opens with a judgment scene. It is probably envisaged as a preliminary judgment; the final, general judgment is described in a later vision in the series (20:11-15). The description of this preliminary judgment is remarkably restrained. The number of the *thrones* is not given, nor is the reader told *to whom judgment was committed.* Not everything about the future is revealed. Like what the seven thunders said (10:4), these details remain shrouded in mystery.

Following this mysterious judgment, John sees *the souls of those who had been beheaded for their testimony to Jesus and for the word of God* rise from the dead to reign with Christ for a thousand years. The description of this thousand year reign is very sparse. It is called the *first resurrection* and is apparently a special reward for those who die a voluntary death for the faith. They will be preserved from *the second death*, which is punishment in the lake of fire (20:14). They *shall be priests of God and of Christ, and they shall reign with him a thousand years.* Their role as priests implies their function as mediators between God and Christ, on the one hand, and the rest of humanity, on the other. Both their acting as priests and their reigning with Christ imply that they have authority over others.

This vision interprets the beatitude spoken in the vision of the three angels— . . . "Blessed are the dead who die in the Lord henceforth." "Blessed indeed," says the Spirit, "that they may rest from their labors, for their deeds follow them!" (14:13). The vision of the thousand year reign shows in a figurative way what it means to say that "their deeds follow them."

It is doubtful that this vision ought to be read as a forecast of particular, historical events. It is much too vague and impressionistic for that sort of reading. Rather, it is a story told to shape the present. It claims that what seems to be defeat—submitting to a violent death for the faith—is really victory. Those who share in "the first resurrection" are those who resisted the beast. So those who oppose the will to power without becoming corrupted by it are those who truly reign and who are the true priests. "Truly reigning" and being "true priests" involves exercising a legitimate, authoritative leadership. Such leadership is very different from the arrogant and rigid leadership of counterfeit power.

The vision continues with the loosing of Satan from the pit. Here, once again, the cyclical character of the Apocalypse is apparent. The rebellion of Satan is described yet another time. It is first described as the dragon's attack on the woman (chapter 12), then in his delegating power to the beast who will be his instrument in his war against the woman's seed (chapter 13). He continues his rebellious activity by assembling the kings of the whole world for the battle of the great day of God the Almighty (16:13-14).

The first rebellion of Satan is quelled by Michael (12:7-9). But the victory is only partial. Satan is defeated in heaven but he reigns on earth. The second rebellion is crushed by another angel (20:1). This time Satan is banished from earth, but only for a limited time. Satan's third and final rebellion consists of assembling the armies of Gog and Magog and instigating their attack on *the camps of the saints and the beloved city* (20:8-9). This final rebellion is suppressed by heavenly means also—*fire came down from heaven.* This time the defeat of Satan is definitive. He is *thrown into the lake of fire and sulphur where the beast and the false prophet were,* where he will be tormented forever.

Some commentators think that this vision was included here simply so that John could work in the fulfillment of Ezekiel 38-39 somewhere in his timetable of the events of the end. Such a rationale is unlikely. Rather, the repeated rebellions of Satan impress on the reader the irrepressible character of the forces of evil and chaos. The implication is that creation and order, peace and justice are quite fragile and partial states and that they are in constant tension with their opposites. The definitive defeat of Satan implies that even though chaos is irrepressible it is less powerful, less real than creative order.

THE LAST JUDGMENT.
20:11-15.

> [11]Then I saw a great white throne and him who sat upon it; from his presence earth and sky fled away, and no place was found for them. [12]And I saw the dead, great and small, standing before the throne, and books were opened. Also another book was opened, which is the book of life. And the dead were judged by what was written in the books, by what they had done. [13]And the sea gave up the dead in it, Death and Hades gave up the dead in them, and all were judged by what they had done. [14]Then Death and Hades were thrown into the lake of fire. This is the second death, the lake of fire; [15]and if any one's name was not found written in the book of life, he was thrown into the lake of fire.

This vision opens with *a great white throne*, which is apparently a special judgment seat; it is a different image from the throne of chapter 4. *(H)im who sat upon it* refers to God in the capacity of universal Judge. The simple statement *from his presence earth and sky fled away and no place was found for them* is the announcement of the end of the world, the destruction of heaven and earth. It is a magnificent statement of the overwhelming majesty and power of the ground of all being, which can destroy as well as create.

The judgment scene itself gives a sense of the radical accountability of all human beings for every deed. It also claims that there is universal justice—*all* are judged according to *what they had done*. The *books* which *were opened* are heavenly records of all the deeds of every human being; they are an image for the conviction that each deed is of ultimate significance and must be accounted for.

The other book is *the book of life* which has appeared several times already in the Apocalypse. Traditionally, the image referred to those who were destined to preserve their physical lives in a particular crisis. Here it is used to designate those who will save "their lives" in a symbolic sense.

The statement that *if any one's name was not found written in the book of life, he was thrown into the lake of fire* seems to exclude human initiative and to deny free will. It seems to imply that those who do good deeds are able to do so simply because they are written in the book.

The *book of life* is an image, not a concept. John has written a vision, not a treatise on free will. The image, *book of life*, refers to salvation from the perspective of providence. It recognizes the mysterious character of our own beings and lives to ourselves, the sense one often has of not being fully in control of one's own destiny. The image does not, however, exclude human choice, intention and effort. When a person behaves unworthily, one's name can be erased from the book (3:5).

The vision expresses two principles of judgment or, to put it another way, two paths to salvation. One is expressed with *the book of life*. The primary sense of the image is that some people are called; they receive special revelation and are expected to live in accordance with it. The other path is expressed in the image of other *books* which are *opened* in the heavenly court. Other people receive no special call or revelation, but their *deeds* are judged rather than their beliefs. The two images are somewhat in tension with one another, but the juxtaposition implies that those who have acted well are in the book of life. In a secondary sense then, the book of life contains the names both of those who have special revelation and live in accordance with it and those who so live even without having the revelation. The Apocalypse's view of the last judgment thus supports the point of view that salvation is possible outside the church.

THE NEW CREATION AND NEW JERUSALEM. 21:1-8.

> **21** Then I saw a new heaven and a new earth; for the first heaven and the first earth had passed away, and the sea was no more. ²And I saw the holy city, new Jerusalem,

coming down out of heaven from God, prepared as a bride adorned for her husband; ³and I heard a great voice from the throne saying, "Behold, the dwelling of God is with men. He will dwell with them, and they shall be his people, and God himself will be with them; ⁴he will wipe away every tear from their eyes, and death shall be no more, neither shall there be mourning nor crying nor pain any more, for the former things have passed away."

⁵And he who sat upon the throne said, "Behold, I make all things new." Also he said, "Write this, for these words are trustworthy and true." ⁶And he said to me, "It is done! I am the Alpha and the Omega, the beginning and the end. To the thirsty I will give water without price from the fountain of the water of life. ⁷He who conquers shall have this heritage, and I will be his God and he shall be my son. ⁸But as for the cowardly, the faithless, the polluted, as for murderers, fornicators, sorcerers, idolaters, and all liars, their lot shall be in the lake that burns with fire and brimstone, which is the second death."

This seventh vision in the last cycle opens with a vision of the new heaven and earth from a negative point of view. The first observation made about the new creation is that *the sea was no more*. This statement is parallel to the eternal confinement and punishment of Satan, the beast and the false prophet. It is also analogous to the remark that "Death and Hades were thrown into the lake of fire" (20:14). The *sea,* like the dragon and the beast, symbolizes chaos. So the elimination of the *sea* symbolizes the complete triumph of creation over chaos, just as the elimination of death implies the complete victory of life over death.

These images should not be taken as descriptions of the way things will be at some future time. Rather, they say that, in a way we cannot fully understand, creation and life do, in the present, have the victory over chaos and death.

Next, the new creation is described from a positive point of view — it contains *the holy city, new Jerusalem, coming down out of heaven from God, prepared as a bride adorned for her husband.* The "husband," as we learn in 21:9, is the Lamb. The image of the city of Jerusalem as the bride or wife of the Lamb has roots in Isaiah 54, a poetic description of the reconciliation of the people with Yahweh. This reconciliation is portrayed as between a forsaken wife, Jerusalem, and her husband, Yahweh. A related image is Jerusalem as the mother of the people (Is 66:6-14).

After these opening views of the new creation, John hears an audition which interprets them. The saying of the *loud voice from the throne* is a new promise which renews some promises from the books of Ezekiel and Isaiah. The promise that God will dwell with the people was made in the book of Ezekiel in the context of the exile after the destruction of the temple and of Jerusalem (Ez 37:26-28). It expresses hope for restoration and was originally temple-centered. The Apocalypse was probably written shortly after the second destruction of the temple and Jerusalem. Here there is no interest in a restoration of the historical city and temple. But there is confidence in the accessibility of God to his people, even during the time of God's apparent absence.

The promise that death would end and that God would wipe away every tear was expressed in Is 25:6-8. These promises are assocated in Isaiah with the image of a great banquet for the future time of salvation. The predictions of an end to death, tears and mourning, like that of an end to hunger, imply that the reality of life is greater and deeper than the reality of death.

Following these anonymous sayings from the throne, words of God are quoted. This is only the second time in the Apocalypse that John explicitly announces words of God; the first was in 1:8. In both passages, the Lord says, "I am the Alpha and the Omega." It is fitting that this saying be placed near both the beginning and the end of the book. It implies that all things in time and space are part of divine providence.

The *thirsty* are promised the *water of life without payment*. Once again, the promise involves an image which has many possible applications. Thirst is an experience common to all people. The implication is that this physical experience points beyond itself to a less tangible craving which is also universal. This craving can be satisfied by the ground of all being for those who seek such satisfaction; the water of life is given freely. To the conquerors, those who sacrifice themselves in time of crisis, the promise given to David is extended (2 Sam 7:14). They too will be sons of God.

The vision closes with a threat of punishment directed against sinners. This saying is not included to encourage the readers to gloat over their enemies. Rather, it is exhortation urging them not to become sinners like those listed. The first two are especially apt for a time of persecution; the faithful are indirectly urged not to be *cowards* or *faithless*.

THE BRIDE, THE WIFE OF THE LAMB.
21:9-22:5,

> [9]Then came one of the seven angels who had the seven bowls full of the seven last plagues, and spoke to me, saying, "Come, I will show you the Bride, the wife of the Lamb." [10]And in the Spirit he carried me away to a great, high mountain, and showed me the holy city Jerusalem coming down out of heaven from God, [11]having the glory of God, its radiance like a most rare jewel, like a jasper, clear as crystal. [12]It had a great, high wall, with twelve gates, and at the gates twelve angels, and on the gates the names of the twelve tribes of the sons of Israel were inscribed; [13]on the east three gates, on the north three gates, on the south three gates, and on the west three gates. [14]And the wall of the city had twelve foundations, and on them the twelve names of the twelve apostles of the Lamb.
>
> [15]And he who talked to me had a measuring rod of gold to measure the city and its gates and walls. [16]The city

lies foursquare, its length the same as its breadth; and he measured the city with his rod, twelve thousand stadia; its length and breadth and height are equal. [17]He also measured its wall, a hundred and forty-four cubits by a man's measure, that is, an angel's. [18]The wall was built of jasper, while the city was pure gold, clear as glass. [19]The foundations of the wall of the city were adorned with every jewel; the first was jasper, the second sapphire, the third agate, the fourth emerald, [20]the fifth onyx, the sixth carnelian, the seventh chrysolite, the eighth beryl, the ninth topaz, the tenth chrysoprase, the eleventh jacinth, the twelfth amethyst. [21]And the twelve gates were twelve pearls, each of the gates made of a single pearl, and the street of the city was pure gold, transparent as glass.

[22]And I saw no temple in the city, for its temple is the Lord God the Almighty and the Lamb. [23]And the city has no need of sun or moon to shine upon it, for the glory of God is its light, and its lamp is the Lamb. [24]By its light shall the nations walk; and the kings of the earth shall bring their glory into it, [25]and its gates shall never be shut by day—and there shall be no night there; [26]they shall bring into it the glory and the honor of the nations. [27]But nothing unclean shall enter it, nor any one who practices abomination or falsehood, but only those who are written in the Lamb's book of life.

22   Then he showed me the river of the water of life, bright as crystal, flowing from the throne of God and of the Lamb [2]through the middle of the street of the city; also, on either side of the river, the tree of life with its twelve kinds of fruit, yielding its fruit each month; and the leaves of the tree were for the healing of the nations. [3]There shall no more be anything accursed, but the throne of God and of the Lamb shall be in it, and his servants shall worship him; [4]they shall see his face, and his name shall be on their foreheads. [5]And night shall be no more; they need no light of lamp or sun, for the Lord God will be their light, and they shall reign for ever and ever.

The seventh vision in the cycle of the seven bowls announced the destruction of Rome, called "Babylon." That announcement was elaborated and interpreted in the "Babylon Appendix" (17:1-19:10). This last cycle of visions has a similar structure. The seventh vision briefly proclaims the descent of the holy city, new Jerusalem (21:2). This proclamation is elaborated and interpreted in the "Jerusalem Appendix" (21:9-22:5).

John's angelic guide and interpreter in the vision of new Jerusalem, the Bride of the Lamb, is one of the seven angels who had the seven bowls. His guide in the vision of the harlot "Babylon" was also one of the same seven angels. This parallelism implies a contrast between the city of Rome and the new, holy city, Jerusalem. Now it is clear from the reference to the historical city of Jerusalem as "Sodom and Egypt" (11:8) that John does not have the restoration of that city in mind here. In fact, it is doubtful that John intended to express something primarily *future* with this vision. We shall look for hints in the description of the city about its significance.

John tells his readers that the angel carried him away in the Spirit *to a great, high mountain* and showed him the city. This remark reminds one of Ezekiel's ecstatic journey to see the restored Jerusalem (Ez 40:1-2). There is no indication here, however, that the city is on a mountain.

The new Jerusalem is described as a perfect cube (vs.16). The cube is a mathematical symbol of perfection like the number seven. The height of the wall around the city is 144,000 cubits, a symbolic number as a multiple of twelve (vs.17). The number twelve had cosmic significance as the number of months in the year. It also had significance in the Jewish tradition as the number of the tribes of Israel.

This description (vss.16-17) is quite similar to Herodotus' (a Greek historian) description of Babylon. If the correspondence is intentional, it is part of the general scheme of correspondences which we have noted. The Lamb and the beast are described similarly; Christ is described as the true Apollo; the mark of the beast is analogous to the seal of

God. The idea here would be that, just as Christ is the fulfillment of expectations attached to Apollo, "Jerusalem" is
the fulfillment of those attached both to the historical
Babylon and its heir, Rome.

In chapter 17, the harlot represented the city of Rome
and the lifestyle associated with it. Here, we have a bride
contrasted with the harlot. In an earlier vision, the temple
and the holy city (Jerusalem) were interpreted as symbols
for the experience of God's presence by the faithful and *not*
as allusions to the physical, historical temple and city
(11:1-2). The images of the bride and the holy city in this
passage should be interpreted in the same way. The description of the wall of the city in vss. 12-14 leads the reader to
such a conclusion. The association of the gates with the
twelve tribes of Israel and of the twelve foundations of the
wall with the twelve apostles of the Lamb implies that the
city is an image for a people. The earthly temple and Jerusalem are destroyed; they have been replaced by the people
living in the presence of God.

The twelve foundations of the wall of the city are adorned
with twelve precious stones. These correspond to the twelve
stones on the breastplate of the High Priest. In John's time,
those twelve stones were associated with the twelve signs
of the Zodiac. Here they are given in reverse order. Re-
versing the usual order may be an intentional device. In
following the Zodiac, people believed that they were in tune
with the heavens and thus with reality as a whole; they
believed they could discern the dictates of fate and then
live in accordance with them. Listing the stones of the
Zodiac in reverse implies that, yes, there is an order in
creation, but it is not what it is commonly thought to be.
It is the church, the people of God, who are truly in tune
with the order of God's universe.

Vs. 22 makes explicit what was already becoming clear—
there is no longer any need for a temple because the people
live in the presence of God and the Lamb. The image
"temple" is still used, even though indirectly, to express
what living in that presence means. Similarly, "sun,"

"moon," and "lamp" are images used to express in an indirect way what it is like to experience *the glory of God* and the presence of *the Lamb*.

Various images from Isaiah 60 are used to describe the glory of the new city (vss. 24-26). Originally these images promised a restored, historical city and nation. Here, they express hope that the truth embodied in the church will one day be recognized by the whole world.

The remark that *nothing unclean shall enter* the city shows that the idea of sacred space is not entirely given up, even though the temple is abolished. But sacred space now includes the whole church, wherever its members are. So sacred space is extended and made people-centered.

Toward the end of the vision, the image of the city is combined with images of a primordial paradise, of Eden (22:1-2). Such images were already used by Ezekiel in describing the restoration. The *river of the water of life* symbolizes the gift of "life," of vitality and joy. The tree of life is here associated with an abundance of food—*twelve kinds of fruit, yielding its fruit each month*—and with healing—*the leaves of the tree were for the healing of the nations*. All of these are world-affirming images for salvation which begin from common types of human experience.

In view of the admonitions and threats in the seven messages, it is clear that the new city is not simply identical with the church at any particular time and place. The particular christian community and the church as a whole, however, ought to be a reflection of this glorious vision. It ought to embody, at least in a partial and anticipatory way, this vision of the destiny of the church.

The radical discontinuity between the old and the new creation implies that there is no linear, progressive relation between human deeds and the fulfillment of these visions of the destiny of the world and the church. John has no ideas of evolution or progress. The destiny of the world and even of the church is beyond human control. But people can discern the outlines of that destiny and ally themselves with it. They can avoid working against it. And they can embody its values in witness to the world.

D. EPILOGUE.
22:6-21.

6And he said to me, "These words are trustworthy and true. And the Lord, the God of the spirits of the prophets, has sent his angel to show his servants what must soon take place. 7And behold, I am coming soon."

Blessed is he who keeps the words of the prophecy of this book.

8I John am he who heard and saw these things. And when I heard and saw them, I fell down to worship at the feet of the angel who showed them to me; 9but he said to me, "You must not do that! I am a fellow servant with you and your brethren the prophets, and with those who keep the words of this book. Worship God."

10And he said to me, "Do not seal up the words of the prophecy of this book, for the time is near. 11Let the evil-doer still do evil, and the filthy still be filthy, and the righteous still do right, and the holy still be holy."

12"Behold, I am coming soon, bringing my recompense, to repay every one for what he has done. 13I am the Alpha and the Omega, the first and the last, the beginning and the end."

14Blessed are those who wash their robes, that they may have the right to the tree of life and that they may enter the city by the gates. 15Outside are the dogs and sorcerers and fornicators and murderers and idolaters, and every one who loves and practices falsehood.

16"I Jesus have sent my angel to you with this testimony for the churches. I am the root and the offspring of David, the bright morning star."

¹⁷The Spirit and the Bride say, "Come." And let him who hears say, "Come." And let him who is thirsty come, let him who desires take the water of life without price.

¹⁸I warn every one who hears the words of the prophecy of this book: if any one adds to them, God will add to him the plagues described in this book, ¹⁹and if any one takes away from the words of the book of this prophecy, God will take away his share in the tree of life and in the holy city, which are described in this book.

²⁰He who testifies to these things says, "Surely I am coming soon." Amen. Come, Lord Jesus!

²¹The grace of the Lord Jesus be with all the saints. Amen.

IT IS NOT immediately obvious who the speaker is who says, *These words are trustworthy and true*. At first, the reader assumes that the angelic guide of the last vision is speaking. But the saying goes on to observe that God *has sent his angel to show his servants what must soon take place*. These words repeat the opening words of the Apocalypse and are clearly meant to refer to the whole book, and not to the last vision alone. The speaker's identity is unimportant.

The next saying, *behold, I am coming soon*, is probably meant to be a saying of Christ (compare 2:16, 3:11). Then a beatitude is given, which in part repeats the beatitude of the prologue. These sayings are collected here near the end of the book, just as two prophetic sayings were attached to the beginning (1:7-8). Their messages are important, even though they are given in the fragmentary way in which they probably were perceived by John.

John himself speaks in vss. 8-9 and communicates an angel's warning against an excessive reverence for the media of revelation. In vs. 10, John still speaks and quotes another saying, probably also by a revealing angel. There is no need for sealing the Apocalypse, since John's visions apply to the present and not to some distant future.

It is not clear whether vs. 11 is a continuation of the saying of vs. 10 or a new saying. In any case, it fits John's expectation that the sinners will not repent (9:20-21) and that the righteous will endure. A series of sayings follow, most of which recapitulate themes of the visions.

John was apparently aware of the creative urges of scribes and editors and thus includes a warning against tampering with his text (vss. 18-19). The warning is backed up with stern threats which are analogous to those made against the leaders criticized in the messages. The proper understanding of reality and of the church's role is at stake.

This warning is followed by another saying of Christ, *Surely I am coming soon,* followed by a response, *Amen. Come, Lord Jesus!* It is impossible to discover what was in John's mind as he wrote those words. He may have understood his own visions in a future-oriented, literal way. But their poetic quality and the fact that a message is expressed in so many *different,* concrete ways imply that John was aware that his visions are pointers, not roadmaps. It is their poetic character and their many levels of meaning that allow them still to be powerful today.

The Apocalypse ends with the typical benediction which closed early christian letters. This ending reminds us that the process of revelation is only complete when the message is applied to the circumstances of a particular congregation.

FOR FURTHER READING.

1. Detailed, scholarly works:

Charles, R. H. *A Critical and Exegetical Commentary on the Revelation of St. John.* 2 vols. The International Critical Commentary. (New York: Charles Scribner's Sons, 1920.)
    This is the classic commentary in English; it is excellent on the subject of John's use of the Hebrew Bible and Jewish tradition.

Collins, Adela Yarbro. *The Combat Myth in the Book of Revelation.* (Missoula, Montana: Scholars Press, 1976.)
    A study of the mythic traditions, the "old stories" used by John, the new meaning his visions gave to them, and how they fit together to create a new work, the Apocalypse.

2. Less detailed, scholarly works:

Caird, G. B. *A Commentary on the Revelation of St. John the Divine.* Harper's New Testament Commentaries. (New York: Harper and Row, 1966.)
    Caird's commentary places the Apocalypse very clearly in its historical setting and also gives the reader a sense of the book as an imaginative, literary creation.

D'Aragon, Jean-Louis. "The Apocalypse." In *The Jerome Biblical Commentary.* Edited by R. Brown, J. Fitzmyer, R. Murphy. (Englewood Cliffs, N.J.: Prentice-Hall, Inc., 1968.) Vol. 2, pp. 467-93.
    A helpful, brief commentary with references to scholarly studies of particular passages.

Harrington, Wilfrid. *Understanding the Apocalypse.* (Washington: Corpus Books, 1969).
    The book begins with an extensive introduction which discusses authorship, literary form, sources, the purpose, the plan, the interpretation and doctrine of the Apocalypse. The comments on individual passages are preceded by quotations of the passage itself and of the pertinent Old Testament texts.

Minear, Paul S. *I Saw a New Earth*. (Washington: Corpus Books, 1968).

    Minear provides three approaches to the Apocalypse. Part I presents the text of the Apocalypse itself divided into sections. Each section is followed by literary analysis, questions for reflection and discussion and suggestions for further study. Part II is a series of essays on significant issues of interpretation. Part III presents the Apocalypse again as a unified whole with brief notes.

3. Theological and pastoral approaches:

Ellul, Jacques. *Apocalypse: The Book of Revelation* (New York: The Seabury Press, 1977).

    A noted French theologian in the Reformed tradition, Ellul offers a profound and challenging theological interpretation of the Apocalypse.

Fiorenza, Elisabeth Schuessler. *The Apocalypse*. Herald Biblical Booklets. (Chicago: Franciscan Herald Press, 1976).

    This booklet argues that the Apocalypse is not concerned primarily with individual, spiritual salvation but that it portrays salvation in universal, political terms. The issues raised by the Apocalypse are related briefly to those raised by theologies of liberation.

Stringfellow, William. *An Ethic for Christians and Other Aliens in a Strange Land*. (Waco, Texas: Word Books, 1973).

    A masterful theological interpretation of contemporary America in terms of the insights of the Apocalypse.

Old Testament Message
A Biblical-Theological Commentary

Editors:
Carroll Stuhlmueller, C.P. and Martin McNamara, M.S.C.

A Michael Glazier Book
THE LITURGICAL PRESS
Collegeville, Minnesota

GOOD NEWS STUDIES

Consulting Editor: Robert J. Karris, O.F.M.

Other Titles in Preparation

NEW TESTAMENT MESSAGE
A Biblical-Theological Commentary

Editors: Wilfrid Harrington, O.P. & Donald Senior, C.P.

"A splendid new series . . . The aim is to mediate the finest of contemporary biblical scholarship to preachers, teachers, and students of the Bible . . . There are treasures to be found in every volume of it."

George MacRae, S.J.

"The stress is on the message, the good news, the *'God-Word'* of the Christian Scriptures."

The Bible Today

"An excellent series of biblical commentaries."

The Catechist

"This series offers new insights and rewards."

Sisters Today

"A sane and well-informed series of commentaries which draws on the best of the Catholic tradition and on a wide range of modern biblical scholarship."

Henry Wansbrough, O.S.B.

(See list of titles on back cover.)